Wicked
CAPITOL HILL

AN UNRULY HISTORY OF
BEHAVING BADLY

ROBERT S. POHL

Charleston   London
THE
History
PRESS

Published by The History Press
Charleston, SC 29403
www.historypress.net

All cover images appear courtesy of the Library of Congress.

First published 2012

Manufactured in the United States

ISBN 978.1.60949.587.9

Library of Congress Cataloging-in-Publication Data

Pohl, Robert S.
Wicked Capitol Hill : an unruly history of behaving badly / Robert S. Pohl.
p. cm.
Includes bibliographical references.
ISBN 978-1-60949-587-9
1. Crime--Washington (D.C.)--History. 2. Scandals--Washington (D.C.)--History. 3.
Capitol Hill (Washington, D.C.)--History. 4. Washington (D.C.)--History. 5. Capitol
Hill (Washington, D.C.)--Biography. 6. Washington (D.C.)--Biography. 7. Capitol Hill
(Washington, D.C.)--Social conditions. 8. Washington (D.C.)--Social conditions. I. Title.
HV6795.W3P64 2012
364.109753--dc23
2012003705

Contents

For Antonia and Ian, of course.

Introduction

Perched high on the hill overlooking the National Mall, the Capitol of the United States towers over the buildings surrounding it, its wide wings embracing the neighborhood. As a symbol of government, it is powerful. Its classical architecture projects permanence. The broad stairs in front and back welcome all to see what goes on behind its marble walls. Even the white of its dome suggests the purity of the actions of those who work inside.

It is unfortunate that the deeds of those within so often fall short of the ideals displayed without. Unfortunate, that is, for those involved. For everyone else, the sight of a congressman—or woman—failing has brought much joy.

Numerous books have been written about this phenomenon and seek to connect the American love of scandal with an explication of national character. The bookshelves groan with weighty tomes that seek to make logical sense of this strange morass of public indignation. Careers have been made by those who can elucidate the Teapot Dome scandal, or Watergate, or Abscam. The books thus written are in turn enlightening and infuriating.

This is not one of those books.

This book intends only to amuse and to divert. The stories presented are those that have shown themselves to be the most entertaining, with special emphasis on those in which some high-flying careerist is brought low because of his peccadilloes.

It is also not entirely about scandals, if scandal is defined as misbehavior that the perpetrator would rather not be generally known but became public

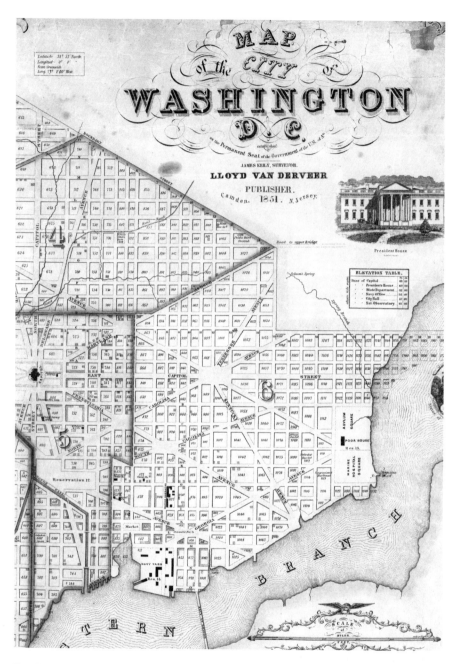

Detail of Lloyd van Derveer's 1851 map of Washington, D.C., showing Capitol Hill. *Library of Congress.*

The Capitol in a snowstorm. January 8, 1939. *From the Harris and Ewing collection. Library of Congress.*

knowledge anyway. Indeed, many of the instances described herein did not raise the level of public outrage to the point that the word "scandal" applies, but rather, they are those whose entertainment value is high enough to merit inclusion.

Although a large number of the scandals have to do with the misbehavior of those who serve in the legislative branch of the United States government, to limit the scope of this book would mean missing out on many wonderful stories perpetrated by those who live in the Washington neighborhood referred to as Capitol Hill. This neighborhood is, by the broadest definition, about four square miles and covers ground from 1st Street NW/SW to the Anacostia River on the south and east and up to Florida Avenue on the north. More restrictive definitions, particularly for the Capitol Hill Historic District, exist as well, but for purposes of this book, we will go with a broader reading.

This particular hill was just one of many low rises in the landscape surrounding the confluence of the Potomac and Anacostia Rivers until one day in 1791, when Peter L'Enfant, who had been tasked with laying out a new city on the site selected by President George Washington, came across it and decided that it was a "pedestal waiting for a monument," as he wrote in a letter to Washington.

L'Enfant also managed to become embroiled in the first scandal on the Hill when he took on Daniel Carroll, one of the large landowners who owned the majority of the city-to-be. Carroll had built a house on a plot of land that L'Enfant had deemed part of one of his avenues, so L'Enfant reacted as only he could: he had it torn down. Needless to say, this did not go over well with Carroll, and his complaints brought swift retribution to L'Enfant, who was sacked from his position.

This event set the tone for the years to come, and whether it was scuttlebutt delivered over the backyard fence or events of national import that were screamed across the pages of newspapers across the country, there has been a steady stream of stories worthy of inclusion in this volume.

Chapter 1

The House of Representatives

When the members of the federal government arrived in Washington, D.C., in November 1800, the city was barely ready for them to get to work. Of the major buildings needed for running the country, only one was even close to completed. The White House, for instance, would remain uninhabitable for a number of weeks, during which time President John Adams found himself in one of the rough-hewn boardinghouses that had sprung up around the Capitol.

From his new digs, Adams could watch builders under the direction of James Hoban add the finishing touches to the new home of Congress—or at least a part of it.

Looking at the outside of the Capitol today, there are five major sections to the building: two large wings north and south, which house the Senate and House, respectively; then the central section surmounted by its grand dome; and finally, two small connecting pieces between the wings and the center.

Of these five, only one was ready by the time the Sixth Congress arrived in D.C. to take up its second session. What is today the connector between the central dome and the northern, Senate, wing had been completed to the point where the Senate could begin its work.

It could have, that is, had they had a quorum. As it was, only fifteen of the thirty-two members had arrived by November 17, the date that their work was to begin, and it would be another four days before there were enough senators there so that they could get to work.

Life was considerably more difficult for their colleagues in the lower house. As the wing of the Capitol planned for their use had not yet even been

The Capitol shown as it was when the federal government arrived in November 1800.
Watercolor by William Russell Birch. *Library of Congress.*

begun, they had to beg the Senate for space. Fortunately, the Capitol had
been designed with future expansion in mind, so there was a room within
the Senate wing that was as yet unused, and so the 106 members of the
House of Representatives were able to get to work themselves—in fact, they
managed to have a quorum three days before the Senate.

During 1801, Hoban recommended that a temporary structure be erected
to give the representatives their own home. President Jefferson concurred,
and during the summer recess of 1801, a building was quickly slapped
together on the ground planned for the House of Representatives.

When the representatives of the Seventh Congress convened, they must
have thought they were the butt of a fairly bad joke. The building they were
expected to convene in was a single-story round wooden structure of such
rickety construction that it required struts all the way around to keep it from
collapsing. A 1914 history of the Capitol summed it up: "The House of
Representatives sat in some peril of their lives, for had not the walls been
strongly shored up from without, the structure would have crumbled to pieces."

For the next three years, as they discussed the Louisiana Purchase,
reorganized the federal courts and recognized the state of Ohio, the

representatives survived in this temporary structure, which they gave the name "The Oven," both for its shape as well as the temperatures that reigned within during the D.C. summers.

Finally, in 1804, they were allowed to move again—back to the same room in the Senate wing that they had abandoned three years earlier. While they continued their work crammed into this ever-tighter space—there were now 139 congressmen—work proceeded on their permanent home. Finally, on October 26, 1807, when the Tenth Congress convened, its 142 members found themselves in their own marble-clad halls.

Their relief was short-lived. On August 24, 1814, during the occupation of Washington by British troops, the Capitol was burned down. Fighting against the tide of opinion that would have sent the government elsewhere, D.C. residents banded together and built a temporary brick Capitol that was used for the next five years while the Capitol was rebuilt.

If the representatives were pleased and relieved that the Capitol was finally accessible to them again when they moved into it in 1819, they certainly had an odd way of showing it. A visitor to the United States who observed life in Washington, D.C., had the following to say about the state of its furnishings:

> *Both houses are handsomely carpeted; but the state to which these carpets are reduced by the universal disregard of the spittoon with which every honourable member is accommodated, and the extraordinary improvements on the pattern which are squirted and dabbled upon it in every direction, do not admit of being described. I will merely observe, that I strongly recommend all strangers not to look at the floor; and if they happen to drop anything, though it be their purse, not to pick it up with an ungloved hand on any account.*
>
> *It is somewhat remarkable too, at first, to say the least, to see so many honourable members with swelled faces; and it is scarcely less remarkable to discover that this appearance is caused by the quantity of tobacco they contrive to stow within the hollow of the cheek. It is strange enough too, to see an honourable gentleman leaning back in his tilted chair with his legs on the desk before him, shaping a convenient "plug" with his penknife, and when it is quite ready for use, shooting the old one from his mouth, as from a pop-gun, and clapping the new one in its place.*

The author was Charles Dickens, who visited the United States in 1842, and the book, *American Notes for General Circulation*, which included the above

Cleaning spittoons outside the Capitol, 1914. *From the Harris and Ewing collection. Library of Congress.*

quote, was published on his return to England. British readers may well have been appalled by this description, but for Americans, it was just another day. It took more than a few globs of spit to discomfit them.

Another American custom that, much like spitting, gradually disappeared in the nineteenth century was dueling. Though it took until late in the century to finally disappear from public life, dueling was already being banned in many places when one of the most famous duels, and the only to feature two sitting congressmen, was fought on February 24, 1838, between Jonathan Cilley of Maine and William Jordan Graves of Kentucky.

The root of the quarrel had been in a speech given by Cilley on February 20 of that year, in which he had said—among a number of other things—"It…must be remembered that the newspapers charge that General James Watson Webb, editor of the *Courier and Enquirer*, of New York received a bribe of $52,000 for his advocacy of the re-chartering of the bank of the United States."

Webb had accused numerous congressmen of corruption, and it was to this charge that Cilley was responding. The editor was, understandably, extremely annoyed at this and jumped on a train to Washington to demand satisfaction.

He had William J. Graves, congressman from Kentucky and a personal friend of Webb's, deliver a note expressing his dissatisfaction. Cilley refused to accept the note on the grounds that he was not personally acquainted with Webb. When Henry Clay, elder statesman, senator from Kentucky and, like Graves, a member of the Whig Party, heard of this refusal, he told Graves, "Go back and tell the --- Yankee that it isn't a challenge, that it is merely a note of inquiry."

After Cilley refused the note a second time, Clay told Graves that this was a personal insult and thus grounds for Graves to demand a duel with Cilley.

Representative Cilley being carried away from his duel with Representative Graves. Detail of painting by Sidney H. Riesenberg, first published in the *New York Tribune*, December 6, 1914. *Library of Congress.*

This was perhaps the best outcome for Webb, not only because he would not personally be at risk during the duel but also because Graves was a well-known marksman and far more likely to prevail over Cilley.

Cilley, whose upbringing in Maine, study of law and subsequent newspaper and political career had done little to teach him about guns, was facing a man who was well versed with firearms. Furthermore, though both combatants had agreed to using rifles, Cilley's weapon was of small bore, while Graves had the use of a powerful weapon.

The next morning, the two parties and their seconds—friends of the duelists who were along to ensure that the agreed-upon rules of the duel were adhered to—set out for Maryland, as dueling had been forbidden in the District of Columbia. On a frozen field just outside the district limits, the seconds paced off eighty paces and the duelists took their places and fired. Graves's first shot went wide, while Cilley purposefully shot into the ground not ten feet from where he stood. This would have, under ordinary circumstances, been the end of it, but Graves insisted on shooting again and, when this still left both combatants standing, a third shot. Graves's final shot hit Cilley in the leg, and he went down. He was dead before his second could reach him.

There was one positive result from this tragedy. The next year, Congress passed "an Act to prohibit the giving or accepting, within the District of Columbia, of a challenge to fight a duel." Although this did not entirely stop dueling—as late as 1859, a U.S. senator was killed in a duel—it did make it less socially acceptable and helped the practice die out.

Washington's position as a new city had more effects on Congress than simply failing to provide accommodation for the congressmen when they arrived. There was also a shortage of infrastructural institutions, such as banks. In order to receive their salaries, congressmen were forced to go the mile and a half down Pennsylvania Avenue to the Treasury Department and have their tellers pay out cash. Given the state of the roads at the time, this was far more arduous than necessary, and furthermore, since all members of Congress had to make the same trek, it made sense to delegate this job to someone else.

For the House of Representatives, this task fell to the Sergeant at Arms. The Sergeant at Arms was originally hired to be the law enforcement officer for the House and to ensure the safety of all those who worked and visited the House side of the Capitol. As his jobs multiplied, the Sergeant at Arms hired on a cashier to take over his role of treasurer to the congressmen.

This system worked fine until November 30, 1889. On that day, the Sergeant at Arms's cashier, a man with the name Craven E. Silcott, went—as always—to the Treasury with a set of certificates on which each member's salary was noted. The certificates had been signed by the clerk of the House. Attached to each certificate was a receipt signed by the member, indicating that the money had been received. Silcott was given some $133,000 in cash, as well as a few Treasury checks. He then distributed some of it, left some in the safe in his office and helped himself to the $10,000 he owned in this safe, as well as the same sum belonging to the Sergeant at Arms, one John P. Leedom. Silcott then announced that he needed to go to New York to have some papers signed. The last communication from him was a pair of telegrams to his wife and to Leedom stating that he had been unexpectedly detained.

And with that, Silcott disappeared. Reaction was swift and furious, with the *National Tribune*'s article titled "A Public Thief and Great Scoundrel" leading the way. Silcott was, according to the *Tribune*, "a man of somewhat shady reputation" who had nonetheless managed to convince Sergeant at Arms Leedom of his honesty.

Silcott was married and had a child, and all three lived together just four blocks from the Capitol. In spite of this domesticity, Silcott had taken up with "a disreputable woman whom he had taken from a bagnio south of the Avenue," and it was with her that he was presumed to have scarpered. It furthermore turned out that Silcott was known to frequent "pool-rooms, houses of ill repute and race-tracks, and has been known to wager large sums of money on horses and various games of chance."

Silcott presumably timed his disappearance knowing that Leedom's term as Sergeant at Arms—and thus presumably his own as cashier—was about to come to an end. Leedom stepped down on December 2, just before the new Republican majority elected one of its own to oversee the security of the chamber.

Where Silcott was now remained a matter of speculation, though the most common guess was Canada, as that would have left him well out of the reach of the long arm of the law. The *New York Herald* published a story on January 31 of the next year claiming it had interviewed Silcott and that he was staying with his paramour's father, a Mr. Thibault, in Terrebonne, Quebec. Silcott denied all wrongdoing, insisting that he had not actually stolen any money and that he had passed on all the money to House members in New York. Furthermore, he claimed that he had not actually won any money on horse races but rather had lost quite a bit. In fact, he claimed that he had only gone to the races to be with those members of Congress who were now accusing him of theft. How these last two statements were likely to make him appear less guilty was not explained.

Finally, Silcott insisted, "The day will come when I will not appear as black as I am now painted." Nonetheless, he showed no interest in returning to Washington to explain in person how innocent he, in fact, was.

A month later, the *New York Times* reported that Silcott had been captured in southwestern Washington State, but that appears to have been a false report. In truth, neither Silcott nor Ms. Thibault was ever seen again. After much discussion and hand-wringing—as well as the revelation that a large number of representatives had no interest in finding Silcott, as they owed him large sums that they were not going to have to return, under the circumstances—the House voted to make good the money that Silcott had stolen.

The House had done far too little to prevent the repeat of such a scandal, and this was made abundantly clear in 1947. As the Republicans prepared to take over the House for the first time since 1930, they elected a new

Representative Alphonse Roy receiving a check for back wages from Kenneth Romney, (right). Roy had won the first district of New Hampshire by just a few votes, and it had taken five months for the election to be resolved. *From the Harris and Ewing collection. Library of Congress.*

Sergeant at Arms, one William F. Russell, whose first job was to look into the finances of the office he was taking over. The previous Sergeant at Arms, Kenneth Romney, was to be appointed Assistant Sergeant at Arms, but this nomination was held up when Russell discovered massive irregularities in the books. Most egregious were a number of checks written by John H. Smithwick, who had been a congressman from 1919 until 1927. In spite of Smithwick having been voted out of office, Romney had cashed a number of checks for him in 1930 and 1931, none of which had ever been redeemed. As far as Romney's accounting was concerned, the checks themselves were assets of the Sergeant at Arms and thus his books were in order.

Russell, unsurprisingly, did not agree. Romney was indicted for fraud to the tune of $143,863. During the trial, it came out that Romney had been trying for years to pay off Smithwick's bounced checks, as well as $25,000 stolen by another cashier. His method was simple: hire friends and have them kick back part of their salary, which would then be used to gradually reduce the missing funds. Unfortunately for Romney, the missing sums were so large that it would have taken many more years to actually cover all the losses.

The judge in his case eventually came to the conclusion that Romney had simply been a patsy for Smithwick and sentenced him to one to three years in jail. After his appeal failed, Romney served only one year. He died three years after being released.

Forty years after Romney's death, it became clear that, once again, the House of Representatives was failing to adequately police itself. The banking scandal of 1992 revolved around the enormous number of checks that members had written that were not covered.

Not all scandals were as dramatic. Some of them turned on something as simple as a letter.

Stephen Joseph Kubel was happy in the spring of 1911. A grand house at 10th and East Capitol Streets, a wife with whom he had recently celebrated his silver anniversary, a daughter in her last year at Eastern High School, a son currently at sea after rounding out his studies in Germany, numerous investment properties and twenty years as chief engraver at the U.S. Geological Survey gave him every reason to be content. It was, therefore, quite a shock when his daughter showed him a letter sent to her from a strange man stating, "I hope I will get to meet you some time."

The letter further stated that it was her picture in the paper that had prompted his writing. From today's perspective, the missive is hardly scandalous. However, this was 1911 D.C., and writing to a young woman to

Above: The fateful picture that so entranced Abraham Lafferty. It was published in the *Washington Times* of May 6, 1911, under the title "Eastern High School Girls Who Take Prominent Part in Irish Fairy Play Tonight for School Art Fund." Florence Kubel is in the center. *Library of Congress.*

Below: Representative Abraham Lafferty as a member of the Vigilant Baseball Club team, 1911. *Library of Congress.*

whom you had not been properly introduced was simply not done, even if you were—as he also stated in his letter—"a bachelor without any family of my own." And this was particularly not done if you were a member of the House of Representatives: the author of the letter, Abraham Walter Lafferty, had been representing Oregon's Second District for just over two months when he sent the incriminating letter.

Although Kubel was deeply angered by the affront displayed in the letter, he decided not to confront the writer while in the midst of his righteous indignation. Instead, he waited a few days before stopping by Lafferty's office, intent on "properly punishing" him. Finding Lafferty to be much smaller than he himself, he contented himself with extracting a letter of apology—not to Miss Kubel but to her father.

In the letter, Lafferty claimed that he had, indeed, noted Miss Kubel's beauty in a picture of her but that the letter sent to her had been done so by his staff, who were concerned about his bachelor status and wished to do something about it.

Later, Lafferty would change his story, claiming that he had actually sent out a large number of letters to various people and that the letter to Kubel was thus not to be taken all too seriously. This was after another letter had arrived in Lafferty's office. Purporting to be from the elder Kubel, it "threatened violence" upon the representative, who had replied that he was available every day from noon to one o'clock for "any punishment Mr. Kubel cared to, and was able to inflict." It was later determined that this letter had been sent from Portland, Oregon, and was simply an attempt by Lafferty's political enemies to re-ignite a scandal that had thus far not managed to gain any public airing whatsoever.

Upon the disclosure of these new charges, various newspapers took up the challenge, including the *Medford Mail Tribune*, which titled its screed "Political Fakir, Street Masher and Cheap Liar," in which it referred to the representative as "Congressman A.W. (Romeo) Lafferty" and did not let up until it had insisted that the "A" stood for Ananias, the early Christian who had achieved infamy for being struck dead for lying.

Why Lafferty, who managed to be reelected to the House—though from a different district—deserved this particular epithet was not further explained by the editor of the *Mail Tribune*. After his second term, he was ousted in the primary and returned to Oregon and his first love: suing the federal government.

Miss Kubel was otherwise untouched by the scandal and was free to marry—and become further embroiled in scandal. Within a few years, she met John Semer Farnsworth, who was a midshipman at the U.S. Naval Academy in Annapolis. They were soon engaged to be married and set a date for November 1915. Farnsworth was, however, assigned to the battleship USS *Michigan*, which was due to sail, and a ship waits for no man, even if he is to get married, so the young couple decided to move up their wedding date to October 20.

For the next twelve years, all seemed well with the Farnsworths. While Mr. Farnsworth launched his career, his wife was "much sought as a guest at all the season's social functions," and she followed him from D.C. to China, back to D.C. and on to California, having four children along the way. Even after the war, he stayed in the navy and became an aviator, following in the footsteps of Florence's brother, who had served in the air service during the war.

In the early twenties, the couple split up and later divorced. Kubel and her children moved back to her father's place in D.C., while Farnsworth began to have money problems, which he attempted to solve by borrowing from an enlisted man—unacceptable in its own right—and then refusing to pay back the money when confronted.

In 1927, the navy decided that it had had enough, and after a court-martial, Farnsworth was found guilty and dishonorably discharged. This hardly solved Farnsworth's money troubles, and he came by a new way of making money: espionage. Relying on old friends who would allow him to read—and even borrow—secret documents, Farnsworth would make copies and sell them to the Japanese. Eventually, friends of his became suspicious, and he was placed under surveillance. On July 16, 1936, he was arrested.

Even though Kubel and Farnsworth had been separated for about fifteen years at this point, Kubel found herself dragged back into this scandal as well. Just before his arrest, Farnsworth had come to D.C. to visit Kubel and their children. When the scandal broke, Kubel moved her children out of the city for a time to avoid the unwanted attention.

Farnsworth was eventually sentenced to four to twelve years in prison, in spite of a long, drawn-out court procedure that went all the way to the Fifth Circuit Court of Appeals, and he ended up serving eleven.

When he was released in the late 1940s, he moved to New York, where he died a few years later. Florence Kubel Farnsworth stayed in the D.C. area and lived to the ripe old age of eighty-two. Her obituary speaks of her four children, twenty-one grandchildren and eleven great-grandchildren but makes no mention of her husband. And she never forgave Representative Lafferty, either—much to the amusement of her family.

Money has always been a source of trouble on Capitol Hill, and numerous congressmen have had their careers upended by their need for more. One of the more egregious stories in this regard was that of Representative Thomas of New Jersey.

J. Parnell Thomas with members of the House Un-American Activities Committee in December 1938. Thomas is on the far right. *From the Harris and Ewing collection. Library of Congress.*

John Parnell Thomas won his election to Congress in 1936, in spite of the enormous Democratic wave that coincided with Franklin Delano Roosevelt's reelection. Throughout his five terms in office, he was a constant critic of FDR's New Deal, consistently arguing that it was going to turn the United States into a Communist country. When the Republicans swept into power in the 1946 elections, Thomas was made chairman of the infamous House Un-American Activities Committee (HUAC). The committee had only recently been made permanent, and Thomas became the first Republican leading it. Under his guidance, the committee investigated Communist propaganda being produced in Hollywood, including questioning such luminaries as Walt Disney, Ronald Reagan, Ring Lardner Jr. and Dalton Trumbo. The latter two, along with eight others, refused to answer any questions, citing the First Amendment of the Constitution, and were later cited for contempt of Congress and jailed. The other famous investigation of HUAC at this time was that of Alger Hiss, whom Whittaker Chambers accused of being a Soviet spy. Although never convicted of this charge, Hiss was convicted of perjury for having lied to Congress.

Thomas's world came crashing down on August 4, 1948. An article by Drew Pearson accused Thomas of hiring Myra Midkiff, ostensibly as a stenographer, though she did not actually have to appear for work at all. All she had to do was kick back her $1,200 salary directly to him. This not only gave his salary a 12 percent boost, but this money was taxed at a much lower rate than the congressman would have had to pay. After Midkiff was married, Thomas found another woman to take her place. Arnette Minor was added to his staff at a salary of $1,800, all of which (after taxes—Thomas was most scrupulous when it came to taxes) found its way into Representative Thomas's pockets. Finally, after that had run for a month and a half, Thomas added a Mrs. Grave Wilson to his payroll, this time at the heady pay of $2,900 a year. Once again, Mrs. Wilson came nowhere near Thomas's office, instead living in Allendale, New Jersey, where Representative Thomas's wife and her sisters took care of her, their elderly aunt.

Unsurprisingly, Pearson's article opened an enormous can of worms for Thomas, and further articles, such as one entitled "New Thomas Charges Are Aired," hardly helped. Finally, Thomas struck back. Even as Attorney General Tom Clark prepared his case for the grand jury, Thomas claimed, in a letter to Clark, that this was nothing but "a new low in politics" and insisted that all of this was due to his work on HUAC and that Clark had himself "coddle[d] rather than prosecute[d], the Communist traitors and conspirators who threaten the very security of the United States." He also called Clark the attorney general for a "defeated and discredited administration."

As it turned out, it was Thomas who was discredited. Although he managed to hang on to win his district in the midst of a Democratic landslide, it was with a much smaller margin than in his previous victories. Three days after the election, an even more serious allegation was published: Thomas had managed to get a number of fighting-age men out of the army in the midst of World War II in return for large campaign contributions. Four days later, he was indicted on the payroll conspiracy. Thomas delayed his trial for almost a year by claiming that he was ill, though a report on his condition prepared by two doctors found him not only well enough to stand trial but also able to enjoy "two to three highballs before dinner and three to four cigars daily."

At his trial, Thomas avoided answering questions by invoking the Fifth Amendment, exactly the tactic he had deplored when used by witnesses before his committee. Nothing helped. In short order, Thomas was convicted and on December 9, 1949, began serving a six-to eighteen-month sentence. He resigned his post, effective January, so for almost a month, a sitting representative was incarcerated. In a final twist, he served his sentence in the same prison where two of the Hollywood Ten had served their time.

Representative Thomas was hardly the only congressman to be brought down by a woman on his payroll. Wayne Hays, representative from Ohio, found out the hard way the fury of a woman scorned. The story broke in 1976 when a reporter for the *Washington Post* received a phone call from Elizabeth Ray. The reporter, Marion Clark, was surprised to hear from this woman, whom she had met a year and a half earlier, but the story she told was riveting, exactly the sort of thing that the *Post* was looking for in this post-Watergate era. Ray told Clark through her tears that she had been on Wayne Hays's payroll for years, ostensibly working for a subcommittee, while her real job was simply to be available for Hays's pleasure at any time. Her reason for turning him in now? He had failed to invite her to his wedding.

Hays was not a well-liked individual. In fact, for over two years, his colleagues in the House had been attempting to rid themselves of his presence. Hays had taken the art of bureaucratic infighting to a whole new level, and from his post running the House Administration Committee, he was able to punish anyone who failed to act the way he wanted. One of his favorite tactics was to turn off the heat in the office of any congressman who crossed him.

Marion Clark shared her information with Rudy Maxa, a fellow reporter, and the two set about turning Ray's confession into a front-page article. On May 23, the article ran under the headline "Closed-Session Romance on the Hill: Rep. Wayne Hays' $14,000 a Year Clerk Says She's His Mistress."

The most damning quote in the story came from Ray herself: "I can't type, I can't file, I can't even answer the phone," and this quote came to epitomize the scandal in the coming years. Ray also mentioned that she was pretty much alone in a fairly large office in the Longworth House Office Building, something that came as a surprise to the dozen or so staffers for Bella Abzug who were crammed into the room next door, a room only slightly larger than Ray's. Ray's room was furnished with an unplugged typewriter, a black leather couch and wall-to-wall carpeting.

As the scandal unfolded in detail in the newspapers, some further evidence came out that cast a slightly different light on the actors. Ray, for instance, was already working on a roman à clef based on her experiences, a novel whose publication date was immediately moved up to cash in on her new notoriety. Furthermore, various people she had worked with earlier testified to her being at least a somewhat-competent secretary.

Nonetheless, the damage was done, and though Hays always maintained that Ray's salary was not just for sexual services, he admitted to most of the charges and resigned on September 1, 1976, to spend more time with his new wife.

Abscam was another one of those scandals that kept reporters busy for months. It involved the attempted bribery, by FBI agents, of various members of Congress. An FBI agent, posing as an Arab sheikh, offered large amounts of money to various congressmen in return for certain favors. In the end, six members of Congress were convicted of bribery and conspiracy.

This is not their story.

Instead, it is the story of the wife of John Jenrette, one of the six convicted of bribery.

Rita Carpenter met John Jenrette when she was the director of opposition research for the Republican National Committee and he was a freshman representative from South Carolina—and a Democrat. In spite of their political differences, they fell in love and married in the fall of 1976. For the next four years, they were the toast of Capitol Hill, throwing elaborate parties, hobnobbing with the movers and shakers of D.C. and attending the requisite political receptions. While he continued his climb, she tried everything from research assistant to singer—her stint at the RNC had ended when she refused their request to spy on her boyfriend—but eventually settled on simply being a political wife.

All of this came crashing down one morning when the Jenrettes' neighbors awoke to the sight of three news trucks parked in front of the Jenrettes' house with all cameras pointed in that direction. Abscam had broken, and it was not long before Jenrette had been convicted, had quit the House and was separated from his wife.

None of this is really relevant to our story, which begins in late November 1980, when it came out that Rita Jenrette was to appear in *Playboy*. A few weeks later, her story appeared in the *Washington Post Magazine*, and then in early March 1981, the April edition of *Playboy* hit the stands. It was full of exactly the kind of dirt one would hope—as well as semi-nude pictures of Jenrette. Claiming at the same time that other congressional wives preferred "gabardine suits and sensible pumps" to her "silky—some said clinging—dresses," but also that she did not "fit into Washington's hot-tub scene," Jenrette saw to it that everyone found something to be outraged by.

One quote in particular has come to epitomize the whole story: "One evening, when the House was in an all-night session, he called to say he

John and Rita Jenrette's house on Capitol Hill. *Photo by Otto Pohl.*

missed me and had to see me. I threw on a coat and walked up to the Capitol portico where John was waiting. He took my hand and led me into the shadows, and we made love on the marble steps that overlook the monuments and city below."

Reactions were swift. Many other Capitol wives denounced her story as a pack of lies, claiming that her stories of sex and drugs in Congress were over-blown, if not entirely manufactured out of whole cloth. Arlene Crane, wife of Representative Phil Crane, even took her to task for her complaints about the sartorial standards displayed on the Hill: "She says she likes silk blouses, and we like tweed suits. Well, I like silk blouses, too."

Jenrette had managed something, however: everyone was talking about her, and she managed to parlay this fame into a book deal, another *Playboy* spread, a brief movie career (appearing in such classics as *Zombie Island Massacre* and *The Malibu Bikini Shop*) and an even briefer career as a singer. She eventually found more steady employment as a correspondent on *A Current Affair*, TV's first tabloid info-tainment show.

In 2009, after a career in real estate, Jenrette married Prince Nicolò Boncompagni Ludovisi of Piombino, thus becoming Princess Rita. Two years later, she was profiled in the *New Yorker*, in which she claimed that the famous scene on the Capitol steps had never happened, that she had simply made that up to live up to her image of a femme fatale.

Whatever the actual truth of the matter, the Jenrettes' tryst on the Capitol steps has ensured that the Jenrettes will remain a part of D.C. lore forever. At least nobody had to die for them to be thus memorialized, in contrast to Representative Taulbee, who is the only representative ever to be killed in the Capitol.

Chapter 2

The Murder of Representative Taulbee

William Preston Taulbee was born to be a politician. Tall, broad-shouldered, handsome and possessing a sonorous voice, his future was assured from the outset. Taulbee grew up on a farm and divided his time between chores and the local school. He married young, and he and the former Miss Lou Emma Oney raised a number of children.

No stranger to hard work, Taulbee's first job was shoveling coal, though he soon abandoned this line of work for a more cerebral one when he went into teaching. He spent six years thus employed. In order to make the most of his voice, Taulbee then became a Methodist minister, while also being a clerk in the county court. During this time, he also studied law and soon opened his own practice, which became quite successful.

With all these pieces in place, Taulbee felt ready to tackle electoral politics on a higher level. His father had recently been elected state senator, but Taulbee was destined for even greater things. On August 14, 1884, Taulbee was unanimously nominated to run as the Democratic candidate to the House of Representatives for the Tenth District of Kentucky. It was as if this election was tailor-made for him. It was an open seat, as the previous incumbent—who had been redistricted into the district in the first place—was not running again, and Taulbee's Republican opponent, one William L. Hurst, was almost completely unknown. On November 4, even as Grover Cleveland was eking out one of the tightest victories in a presidential election, Taulbee sailed home with a vote margin of over two thousand.

The House of Representatives in 1890. Photograph by Charles M. Bell. *Library of Congress.*

At first, Taulbee's future as a politician seemed golden. Accolades such as "silver-tongued" were routinely attached to his name, his bearing was given as "dignified and impressive" in spite of his youth, his addition to the Kentucky delegation ensured that "Kentucky will regain her lost influence in legislation" and he was soon routinely referred to as "Our Pres." At least two families went so far as to name their child "Pres Taulbee." Only the *Catlettsburg Democrat* wrote anything that could be called remotely ominous: "We will now say in print what we have predicted to various gentlemen in private, That Pres. Taulbee, *should he live*, will be governor of Kentucky inside of ten years." (Emphasis added.) And as to the possible source of his downfall, an article in the *Daily Bulletin* of Maysfield, Kentucky, pointed out that his speech, which had been delivered before a full house, had been "largely composed of ladies," quite surprising in these pre-suffrage days.

Nonetheless, eventually the normal, day-to-day grind of governing began to show, and with it, complaints about Taulbee's handling of this and that issue crept into the newspaper. When it came time for reelection, Taulbee realized that he could hardly count on the same level of support he had in the last election. In spite of running against the same opponent—and this time as an incumbent—Taulbee saw it necessary to engage Hurst twenty-seven times all across the district. For the better part of the month, these two worthies took their show on the road and delivered dueling speeches—each an hour long—to audiences all across the Tenth District.

On election day, Taulbee—in contrast to many of his Democratic colleagues around the country—prevailed, although with a much smaller margin than he had claimed two years earlier.

The model room of the Patent Office, where William Taulbee and Laura Dodge were caught "in flagrante or thereabouts." *From the Brady-Handy Collection. Library of Congress.*

It was almost immediately after his return to Washington that the tone of articles about Taulbee began to change. Within a few months of the start of the new session, rumors that he would not run for reelection began to fly, and Taulbee's buying of a house and announcement that he would stay in D.C. even after retiring from Congress did nothing to quash these stories.

The real scandal broke in December of that year. As so often is the case, the first inkling of something happening was quite minor. A short article in the *Washington Post* indicated that "a Congressman from Kentucky" had been caught "in a very compromising position." He and a young girl, described as a "petite blonde employee of the Patent Office," had been discovered by Richard C. Gill of the Patent Office. The young woman had run off in one direction and the Kentucky congressman in another.

The next day, an article ran in the *Louisville Times* with the following headline:

> *Kentucky's Silver-Tongued Taulbee Caught in Flagrante*
> *Or Thereabouts, with Brown-Haired Miss Dodge, Also of Kentucky*
> *Congressman and Clerk Lunching on Forbidden Fruit and Hidden Waters*

The headline ended with a question that made clear where the author stood on the matter: "What's the World Coming To?"

Although without a byline, it was clear that it could have written by only one man: Judge Charles E. Kincaid. In spite of his title, his job was the Washington correspondent of the *Louisville Times*. It had not taken him long to determine the identity of either the Kentucky congressman or his paramour. When the former refused to comment on the situation, Kincaid tracked down the latter.

He found Laura L. Dodge living with her parents on Capitol Hill, just a few blocks east of the Capitol. She was, in Kincaid's words, "a little beauty, bright as sunshine and saucy as a bowl of jelly. She is petite of figure, but plump as a partridge. Her hair is brown, her eyes blue, cheeks like peaches, lips like rosebuds dipped with dew."

She was also eager to talk and freely admitted that she was not from Kentucky, contradicting her appointment to the Patent Office, which had stated that she was. When Kincaid asked where she was, in fact, from, she refused to answer on the grounds that she did not wish to get Mr. Taulbee into trouble, as he was "a gentleman and I am supposed to be a lady. We will both swear on a stack of Bibles that we have not done anything."

Kincaid concluded his article: "What a mess this is for an ex-Methodist minister and a Congressman from the grand old Commonwealth of Kentucky."

The Capitol as it looked during William Taulbee's time on the Hill. *Library of Congress.*

Unsurprisingly, the newspapers in Kentucky repeated Kincaid's story. More surprising, however, was that none of the other newspapers in D.C. followed suit. In fact, the *Washington Post* did not even bother following up on its story by, say, mentioning which representative had been thus caught. The story had ended with the note that Patent Commissioner Benton J. Hall was making his own investigation; what came of this was never printed, anywhere. Finally, when it came to the end of the congressional term and the *Post* published an article entitled "Men Who Quit Congress," Taulbee was featured prominently, but his scandal was not mentioned with one word.

In short, it was remarkable how quickly this scandal became yesterday's news. What bothered people in Kentucky most was Miss Dodge's lie about being from Kentucky, but with her move to another job at the Pension Office, even this line of attack fizzled out. In November, Taulbee's candidate lost, as did much of the Democratic Party, so even if Taulbee had won, he would no longer have been in the majority.

Taulbee, for his part, did not appear too put out by his change in fortune; in fact, he may have welcomed the excuse to give up a job that he found himself unsuited to. The fact that one of the first jobs he took on as a lawyer once his term expired earned him about five times his yearly salary as a representative cannot have hurt. Back in Kentucky, Taulbee's new wealth was treated with some satisfaction, and it appeared that he was well on his way to rehabilitating his image, as well as becoming an elder statesman. Just before the election, the Stanford, Kentucky *Semi-Weekly Interior Journal* had gone so far as to announce that Taulbee's support in the race to succeed him would almost certainly be enough to bring victory to his chosen successor, as after all, Taulbee remained "the most popular man in the district."

Taulbee did suffer one setback the first year that he was back in private life, when he was caught up in the House banking scandal of 1889; Taulbee had some of his savings with the Sergeant at Arms and lost them when Cashier Craven Silcott absconded with the money. Where current representatives could hope for a replacement of the missing monies by the government, Taulbee's status was uncertain.

Another even more minor irritant was Charles Kincaid. Since Taulbee continued to spend time in his former place of work and Kincaid remained the *Louisville Times*'s correspondent, the two men met frequently. The run-ins almost always ended badly for Kincaid, who was a foot shorter and considerably lighter than Taulbee, who delighted in tweaking the smaller man, both physically and verbally.

One fateful morning in February 1890, matters came to a head. The exact sequence of events will probably never be determined, but some facts are undisputed. Around 11:30 a.m., just as the House was to go into session, Taulbee and Kincaid met up just outside the House doors. Words were exchanged, with Taulbee apparently requesting a discussion with Kincaid outside, something that the latter was loath to do. Most sources agree that Taulbee said, "I wish to see you" or words to that effect. During this exchange, Taulbee is said to have grasped Kincaid's lapel. Some claimed that Taulbee also tweaked Kincaid's nose.

The *Washington Post* wrote the next day that the altercation ended with the ominous words, "I am in no condition for a physical contest with you—I am not armed," to which Taulbee replied, "Then you had better be."

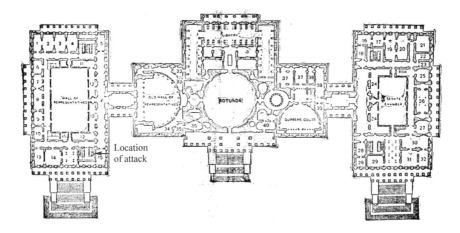

Above: Plan of the Capitol, showing the location of the shooting. *Library of Congress.*

Below: Newspaper portraits of Charles Kincaid and William Taulbee, as well as a line drawing of the actual attack. *Library of Congress.*

Taulbee and Kincaid did indeed meet two hours later, and this time Kincaid was armed. Taulbee, along with Sam Donelson, former Doorkeeper of the House, was descending the stairs outside the House chamber when he heard a voice above him saying, "Can you see me now?"

Taulbee turned and was struck in the face by a bullet fired by Kincaid. Taulbee stumbled but, amazingly, did not fall. He staggered down a few steps, at which point some friends caught him. He was taken to a committee room and from there to Providence Hospital. Meanwhile, Kincaid, who had proudly announced, "I did it; I am the man who did the shooting," was arrested by an officer of the Capitol Police and taken from there to a police station and turned over the Metropolitan Police.

A private room at Providence Hospital, such as the one to which William Taulbee was taken. This picture was taken circa 1895. *Library of Congress.*

At Providence Hospital, it was determined that the wound was non-fatal. The bullet had hit just below Taulbee's left eye and then settled somewhere in the back of the skull. Accordingly, Kincaid was released on $2,000 bond, under the assumption that he could be rearrested if Taulbee did, in fact, die. The newspapers of the time, for their part, had a field day, particularly the Kentucky papers, which did their best to—depending on their attitude toward Taulbee—defend or denounce Kincaid's action. While the *Mount Airy Sentinel-Democrat* was convinced that Kincaid's "coolness and deliberation" indicated that this was murder, plain and simple, other papers, including Kincaid's *Times*, were convinced that Kincaid was entirely innocent.

News for the next week or so was good. Taulbee continued to improve and was able to tell his brother his version the of events: that he had grabbed Kincaid's lapel, that he might have even taken him by the ear but certainly not touched his nose in any way. On March 4, Dr. John W. Bayne was so satisfied with his patient's condition that he went home for the night.

The next day, matters had taken a decided turn for the worse. Far from looking forward to his eventual recovery, the medical staff now was seeing his death as imminent. Shortly after 5:00 a.m. on March 11, Taulbee succumbed to his wound. The immediate cause of death was an abscess that had formed around the bullet, which had come to rest between the brain and the skull. The abscess had then impinged on the brain and paralyzed it.

The news of the death was telephoned to the police headquarters, and a sergeant was dispatched to rearrest Kincaid. It was still early in the morning, so Kincaid asked that he be allowed to sleep an hour longer. This request was denied, however, though Kincaid was given his own cell at police headquarters and allowed to see visitors, including his brother, who was a doctor. Reporters at the time remarked on how poorly Kincaid was doing; the stress of the previous ten days had clearly gotten to him.

Three days after his death, Taulbee's body was laid out at George P. Zurhorst's funeral parlor on Capitol Hill, and a procession, consisting of a delegation from Kentucky as well as a deputation of Masons, wound its way around the Capitol and to the Baltimore and Potomac Depot on the National Mall. Taulbee's coffin was placed on a train west and taken back to Taulbee's hometown of Mount Sterling, Kentucky.

Kincaid was indicted by a grand jury the day after the funeral, at which point he could not "stand alone for one minute." In spite of this, he was kept in jail for another month. Finally, on April 21, he was allowed to make bail of $20,000. Five friends stood by to help him, and that very afternoon, Kincaid walked back out of jail.

It took almost a year before the trial was set, and finally, on March 23, 1891, Kincaid stood in court again. Nothing about the trial was simple; it took two days just to seat the jury.

The district attorney, one Charles C. Cole, did his level best to show that Kincaid had murdered Taulbee, even bringing in a skull to show the exact path the bullet had taken. However, his best witness was clearly Samuel Donelson, the former doorkeeper of the House, who was with Taulbee at the time of the shooting. Donelson was reportedly the source of the *Post*'s quote for Taulbee saying "Then you had better be." Donelson claimed that this was something a Mrs. Mary Wilmore (or Gilmore) had heard Donelson say over the dinner table at his boardinghouse, but under oath Donelson denied ever having said anything of the sort. He added, "I should say, that anything [I] may have said at the boarding-house was hearsay."

Donelson's testimony was otherwise quite straightforward: he had been with Taulbee when the latter was shot, requesting that he join him on the House stairs in order "to avoid a difficulty between himself and Mr. Kincaid." Taulbee took Donelson's hand and asked, "What do you want,

Sam?" Kincaid, from behind and farther up the stairs, called out, "Taulbee, you can see me now," and fired the fatal bullet.

During Kincaid's defense, much was made of the attacks that Taulbee had inflicted upon Kincaid in the time between his outing of Taulbee's relationship with Dodge and the shooting. General Grosvenor, his lead attorney, spoke at length about this during his opening statement: "I will say that Taulbee constantly and in various ways insulted and assaulted this almost helpless man, the shrinking, cowering victim," and as he rose to greater oratorical heights and losing sight of any grammatical niceties, added, "On another occasion while he was passing through one of the iron gates Taulbee dashed him against the iron railing. Kincaid finds himself afterward in the elevator. Suddenly the weight of a boot heel is crushed down on his toe and he is held almost screaming with pain under the giant Taulbee's revenge."

A few days later, Kincaid himself took the stand, reiterating the stories his attorney had told and furnishing his own version of the penultimate run-in with Taulbee. According to Kincaid, it had ended with Taulbee saying, "You damned little coward and monkey, now go and arm yourself."

A week later, the jury was finally given their instructions and retired. They returned that very evening, and shortly before 7:00 p.m. on April 8, they declared Charles Kincaid not guilty, ruling that he had acted in self-defense.

Kincaid immediately went home and collapsed. His health, which had not been good even before he wrote the fateful article in December 1887, had suffered dramatically both because of his feud with Taulbee and from the strain of imprisonment and the trial. Kincaid was only in his mid-thirties when the above events happened, but he lived only another fifteen years, dying at fifty-one years of age.

In doing so, he had managed to outlive Mrs. Taulbee. In spite of stories that she had dumped her husband immediately upon hearing of his infidelities, in truth she stayed with him and returned to Kentucky after his death. She only outlived her husband by thirteen years, dying in 1903 back in Kentucky. She is buried next to her husband.

Miss Dodge managed to survive the affair better than the other three. She had moved from the Patent Office to the Pension Office shortly after her affair became public but was fired from that position in 1895. In September 1900, she married William Albert Paul, a reviewer in the Pension Office who was fifteen years her senior. She moved in with him, a few blocks closer to the Capitol, but still on A Street NE. They later moved to R Street NW.

Paul died in 1927 without issue. The former Miss Dodge later remarried, this time to the attorney Tracy L. Jeffords, who had previously been in charge of both of her parents' wills and had been an assistant U.S. attorney. For the next twenty years, the names "Mr. and Mrs. Tracy Jeffords" were a staple of the society pages of the *Washington Post*. Mr. Jeffords died in 1949, while his wife lived to the ripe old age of eighty-nine years, passing away on December 25, 1959.

Chapter 3

The Senate

The United States Senate has always prided itself on being the more deliberative of the two bodies that constitute Congress. From its vantage point just north of the hurly-burly of the House of Representatives, it has looked down on the larger body and considered itself a brake on the more unruly House. Among the forty-four rules that the Senate has set for itself, there are numerous that deal directly with how senators are to comport themselves, including paragraph two of rule nineteen: "No Senator in debate shall, directly or indirectly, by any form of words impute to another Senator or to other Senators any conduct or motive unworthy or unbecoming a Senator." Paragraph three is even pithier: "No Senator in debate shall refer offensively to any State of the Union."

In spite of its supposedly more contemplative status, the atmosphere in the Senate was just as explosive as in the House—if not more so. Tempers ran particularly high leading to the Civil War, an entirely unsurprising result of the corrosive effects of the slavery debate that was dividing the country. In two cases during the decade before the war, there were actual violent outbursts on the floor.

The first was in 1850, when Thomas Hart Benton, famous Missouri senator and the first senator to serve thirty years in office, made remarks that so enraged his colleague, Henry S. Foote from Mississippi, that Foote pulled out a pistol and waved it at Benton. Carrying a pistol into Congress was hardly unusual back then, though actually threatening a colleague with one was still out of the ordinary.

Above: The scene in the Senate chamber as Henry Wilson is inaugurated as vice president—and thus presiding officer of the Senate. March 4, 1873. From *Frank Leslie's Illustrated Newspaper*, March 22, 1873. *Library of Congress.*

Below: *Scene in Uncle Sam's Senate. 17th April 1850.* Edward Williams Clay's take on what happened during the altercation between Henry Foote and Thomas Benton. *Library of Congress.*

Benton advanced on Foote, saying, "I have no pistols! I disdain to carry arms. Stand out of the way and let the assassin fire!" while Wisconsin senator Augustus Dodge attempted to stop him.

Foote fortunately did not pull the trigger and was instead relieved of his weapon by New York senator Daniel Dickinson. After a few more minutes of discussion, the Senate adjourned for the day. A committee of seven was set up to investigate and in its report, castigated both senators for their actions but declined to recommend any sanction against either of the two.

A far more dangerous altercation occurred on the Senate floor about six years later. In this case, the perpetrators were Charles Sumner, of Massachusetts, and Preston Brooks, of South Carolina. Sumner had spent the last two days attacking the Kansas-Nebraska Act, which effectively repealed the Missouri Compromise and thus reopened the issue of slavery in the Kansas territory. Sumner equated this with the rape of a virgin and, in particular, singled out the authors of the act, Stephen Douglas and Andrew Butler, for his attack.

Sumner began by comparing Butler and Douglas with Don Quixote and Sancho Panza and then moved on to more *ad hominem* attacks, declaring that Douglas had made that "harlot, slavery" his mistress and that Butler—who was still affected by a stroke he had suffered—had "with incoherent phrases discharged the loose expectoration of his speech."

Even as Sumner gave his speech, Douglas is said to have remarked to a colleague that Sumner was liable to be shot by "some other damn fool." In the end, the "other damn fool" was neither Douglas nor Butler but rather Representative Preston Brooks of South Carolina, who also happened to be Butler's nephew. His first inclination was to challenge Sumner to a duel, but upon reflection, he decided that Sumner was not worthy of this course of action and so took matters into hand more directly.

On May 22, 1856, Brooks strode into the almost-empty Senate and approached Sumner, who was quietly working at a desk, and said, "I have read your speech twice over, carefully; it is a libel on South Carolina, and Mr. Butler, who is a relative of mine," and even as he finished speaking, lay into Sumner with his gold-headed gutta-percha cane. Sumner, who was trapped by his desk, received multiple blows while almost completely unable to defend himself. Brooks only broke off the attack when his cane broke, and Sumner was finally able to stagger away, blinded with blood.

Brooks left the chamber unmolested, as two friends who had accompanied him, Representatives Keitt of South Carolina and Edmundson of Virginia, kept all others away by brandishing a pistol.

Lithograph of the Preston Brooks attack on Charles Sumner. South Carolina representative Lawrence Keitt holds up a cane to prevent others from coming to Sumner's defense. The print, which may never have been published, was from John Henry Bufford's shop and may have been by Winslow Homer. *Library of Congress.*

The reactions to this brutal attack were, unsurprisingly, mixed. In Columbia, South Carolina, "A large meeting of the [*sic*] citizens was held sustaining Brook's [*sic*] assault on Sumner," while in Springfield, Massachusetts, "the students of Amherst College held an indignation meeting last evening in reference to the outrage upon Mr. Sumner." The *New York Tribune*, which was decidedly and unabashedly pro-Sumner, also noted the reactions around the country and found that the "*Richmond Whig*, which so loudly applauded the cowardly ruffian Brooks for his assault on Mr. Sumner,...seems...to begin to feel a little the force of public opinion." Although the *Whig*'s editors continued to feel that the attack was, in principle, acceptable, they had come to the conclusion that "Brooks would have done better to have selected the street instead of the Senate Chamber for the scene of action."

The most forceful reaction came from some South Carolinians, who responded by sending Brooks new canes, with the encouragement to finish up what he had started. For a time, D.C. businesses advertised "Brooks canes," about which the Washington correspondent of the *New York Evening Post* quoted a shopkeeper as saying, "Them's the sort they use in Congress."

Brooks was fined $300 after having waived a trial, gone before a judge and argued that he had acted in self-defense. An attempt to expel him from Congress failed, though a motion of censure was passed. Brooks did not have long to celebrate his victory: on January 27, 1857, he died of an inflammation of the throat.

Sumner would remain unable to continue his duties as a senator for three years. At first, his doctors feared for his life, and an attack of erysipelas seemed to doom him. He recovered, however, and took a trip to Europe in hopes that this would cure him. On his return, he found himself still unable to take up his old duties, so a return to Europe was organized, and thus it was not until the fall of 1859 that he was able to return to D.C. and the Senate.

After the turmoil of the Civil War and Reconstruction, there were ever fewer of these attacks. Senators McLaurin and Tillman, however, showed that even with the dawn of the new century, there was still no way of reining in the exuberant natures of some senators.

Benjamin Ryan Tillman and John Lowndes McLaurin were both senators from South Carolina and both Democrats. Their similarities ended there, however. Though McLaurin had initially been mentored by the elder Tillman,

Senators Benjamin Tillman (left) and John McLaurin (right) in a picture from the May 26, 1901 *St. Louis Republic. Library of Congress.*

their political views had lately diverged, and by 1901, they were almost diametrically opposed. At this time, both senators offered their resignation, as they had come to the conclusion that their votes in the Senate were consistently canceling each other out, leaving South Carolina with effectively no voice whatsoever in the Senate. The governor of South Carolina refused to accept the resignations, keeping both in the body. However, the Democratic Party of the state voted to toss McLaurin out of the party.

On February 22, 1902, matters came to a head. Tillman was on the Senate floor during a speech by Senator John Coit Spooner. During this speech, which was about the peace treaty ending the Spanish-American War, Tillman mentioned that his colleague McLaurin had voted in favor of the bill only after being bought off by the assurance of certain patronage jobs in South Carolina. McLaurin, who was not present, was informed of this and came storming onto the Senate floor, declaring that Tillman's statement was "a willful, deliberate and malicious lie."

Before he could finish, Tillman had jumped up, vaulted over several intervening chairs and punched McLaurin in the forehead. McLaurin replied with a "fierce upper-cut," and the two men grappled. They were separated by the Assistant Sergeant at Arms and various other bystanders, including Tillman's son.

The punishment that might be meted out on the two pugilists was the talk of the town for the next few days. Some felt that expulsion was the only appropriate response, while others felt that censure was the correct way to proceed. A number of people felt that a duel would be the result of this contretemps; fortunately, all parties involved soon denied this. Tillman was disinvited from a White House state dinner.

In the end, the two were simply censured. McLaurin served out his term and then did not stand for reelection. Tillman, on the other hand, served another sixteen years and died in office.

There was one upshot of their altercation: paragraph two of rule nineteen, as quoted previously, was passed as an attempt to reduce the likelihood of a repeat performance of what happened on that February day. And while the phrases "my esteemed colleague" and "the great state of" have been spoken drenched in sarcasm over the years, actual physical confrontations on the Senate floor have indeed become a thing of the past.

Senators have consequently had to find other ways of misbehaving, with one of the most widespread being their willingness to listen to lobbyists who are attempting to bend the laws of the United States to their own ends.

Female lobbyists in the marble room of the Senate. Originally published in *Frank Leslie's Illustrated Newspaper* on January 5, 1884. *Library of Congress.*

The lobbyist now has a history stretching back 150 years and remains a Washington fixture in spite of attempts over the years to rein in this influence.

One of the all-time great descriptions of this D.C. creature is by the trailblazing female journalist Emily Edson Briggs, better known as Olivia, who wrote of the lobbyist: "Winding in and out through the long, devious basement passage, crawling through the corridors, trailing its slimy length from gallery to committee room, at last it lies stretched at full length on the floor of Congress—this dazzling reptile, this huge, scaly serpent of the lobby."

This was from 1869, when lobbying flowered into the art form that it has remained ever since. A more remarkable scene was described in an 1883 book:

> *That frosty-headed, red-faced old fellow, who dances with such animation, is Senator ——, who has made great reputation by advocating a reform of the tariff; his speeches always attract marked attention from the galleries;*

his wife is not spending the winter in Washington, preferring to live a quiet life at their country home, which decision is quite agreeable to the senator, as we shall see. Isn't his partner beautiful? Why, she dresses a divine form with the grace such perfect mould deserves. Her smile is sweeter than a siren's lute, and the measure of her step is as infectious as the jig-creating melodies of an expert negro banjoist. How entrancingly she looks up into the senator's red face; the beams of her lovely eyes strike wrinkles of admiration all over the old gentleman's countenance. By careful notice we may see him squeeze her waist with one arm, but the most expert mathematician could not tell which of the two holds the tightest grip with their linked hands.

This woman has the senator in her grasp; what will she do with him? Her character affords the best answer. Two years ago she was an adventuress among Wall street nabobs; she made some money by selling her charms to "bulls" and "bears" for "pointers" on the stock market. Promiscuity soon drove her out of speculation, but having great resource she fell in with a rich Californian, who took her to San Francisco. There she was a "high roller," and by keeping a sharp lookout for the main chance she finally "struck it rich." A coast millionaire, with visions of transcontinental railways in his head, concluded that he could use her with advantage at Washington. He accordingly made her a tempting and acceptable offer, after which he had a bill drafted appropriating millions of public lands to a construction company, of which he was the soul, body and members, to assist in the building of a railroad, projected in his brain. This woman is a professional lobbyist now, and if she succeeds in having the bill passed $50,000 will be her reward. She tackles our venerable senator, because he has made several speeches against the appropriation of any part of the public domain to advance individual interests. His influence, therefore, in advocacy of her bill, will anticipate all opposition and insure an early passage of her measure.

But the full effects of her insinuating grace and magnetism is not [as powerful in] *the ball room as in her boudoir; for there, under the magic of nature's touch, whatever may be the senator's misgivings and compunctions he will swear allegiance with the impassioned eloquence of the sweetest lover.*

This description is from a book entitled *Mysteries and Miseries of America's Great Cities.* How much, if any, of this was true is almost impossible to say. There certainly are not enough facts given to even begin to determine the identity of either the senator or his lobbyist.

Benjamin Perley Poore, for many years a newspaper correspondent in D.C., wrote a more nuanced take on the same situation in his *Reminiscences of Sixty Years in the National Metropolis:*

> *The lobby is a quiet but efficient part of Congressional machinery. Scores of bills are considered and passed during every session, each involving thousands of dollars, and those having them in charge do not feel like turning a deaf ear to any one who can promise support. An occasional investigation reveals the work of ex-Congressmen, who hover about the Capitol like birds of prey, and of correspondents so scantily paid by the journals with which they are connected that they are forced to prostitute their pens. But the most adroit lobbyists belong to the gentler sex. Some of them are the widows of officers of the army or navy, others the daughters of Congressmen of a past generation, and others have drifted from home localities, where they have found themselves the subjects of scandalous comments. They are retained with instructions to exert their influence with designated Congressmen. Sometimes the Congressmen are induced to vote aye on a certain measure; sometimes to vote no, and it often occurs that where the lobbyist cannot make an impression on them, one way or the other, they will endeavor to keep them away from the House when the roll is called.*
>
> *To enable them to do their work well, they have pleasant parlors, with works of art and bric-a-brac donated by admirers. Every evening they receive, and in the winter their blazing wood fires are often surrounded by a distinguished circle. Some treat favored guests to a game of euchre, and as midnight approaches there is always an adjournment to the dining-room, where a choice supper is served. A cold game pie, broiled oysters, charmingly mixed salad, and one or two light dishes generally constitute the repast, with iced champagne or Burgundy at blood heat. Who can blame a Congressman for leaving the bad cooking of his hotel or boarding-house, with the absence of all home comforts, to walk into the parlor web which the cunning spider-lobbyist weaves for him?*

It could hardly be said that the only excitement in the Senate came from the senators themselves. Occasionally, it was the building itself that would launch a hundred headlines.

It was Friday afternoon in May 1876. The Senate had been in session since that morning, deliberating in the trial of William W. Belknap, who was being impeached on charges of corruption. In spite of his having been rapidly and unanimously convicted in the House of Representatives, the Senate had spent almost two months on this case, and there seemed to be no end in sight.

As the discussion murmured on in the Senate, others went about their business. Lyman B. Cutler, a clerk in the Senate's folding office, and John King, a carpenter, descended into a basement storage chamber on some errand. The room was being rebuilt to accommodate more of the papers emanating from the folding office, and the two were supervising the work in some way. One of the two (reports differ) made the mistake of lighting a match.

A terrific explosion ensued, which badly burned Cutler as well as shredded his clothing but otherwise left him remarkably unscathed. King, on the other hand, was thrown against a wall and then struck by shrapnel. He was taken to a nearby hospital but died shortly thereafter from his wounds.

Elsewhere in the Capitol, confusion reigned. The Senate suspended its business briefly while the extent of the damage was assessed. In the aftermath, it was determined that a pipe that supplied coal gas for lighting the Capitol had been found to be leaking into the storage chamber a few days earlier. A plumber had been notified, but no actual repairs had been made. The buildup of gas in the chamber had been ignited by the lit match, causing the explosion.

Fortunately, other than King's death and a great deal of confusion, no further impact on the Capitol was recorded. This had the unfortunate side effect that no further attempts were made to reduce the chance of such an explosion reoccurring. Twenty-two years later, a far more dangerous explosion happened, and it was only sheer luck that no further deaths were to be reported.

Once again, the explosion occurred on the Senate side, this time in the subbasement below the old Senate wing. The explosion "shook the walls of the building and tossed about heaps of stone as a giant's hand might trifle with toys. Flames swept through corridors, and, bursting through the windows, painted a lurid hue upon the walls and cast a glow over the eastern part of the city," as described by the *Washington Times* the next day.

Fortunately, this had all occurred on an otherwise quiet Sunday afternoon, ensuring that only a minimum of people were in the area, and in spite of the massive damage to the building itself—sources claimed that without the rapid intervention of the fire department, the entire building would have been lost—no one was injured. Thomas H. Clark, librarian of the law library stored in the Capitol, arrived with great trepidation about the state of the seventy-five thousand books in his charge. He found them all still in acceptable condition, some with water damage, but nothing that would have reduced the usefulness of the most important law library in the world.

The aftermath of the explosion in the Capitol on July 2, 1915. On the left are the telephone booths that were particularly damaged. *Library of Congress.*

One good thing came from the explosion, as the change to electric lighting in the Capitol, which had been slow in coming due to the insistence of some congressmen that the light from this newfangled technology flickered too much, was rapidly concluded, reducing the chance for further damage from this particular source.

Sadly, it wouldn't be long before another explosion rocked the Capitol. It was just before midnight on July 2, 1915, when a great roar thundered through the building. Capitol police officer Frank Jones, who was on duty at the east entrance, was convinced that the dome of the Capitol had finally collapsed. When he investigated, he discovered the Senate reception room, just outside the Senate floor, in ruins.

It did not take long to discover the source of the blast: three sticks of dynamite. They had been laid by one Erich Muenter, who was attempting to protest the conduct of the United States *vis-à-vis* the European war. In spite of the supposed neutrality of the United States, Muenter felt that public policy had a decidedly pro-British bent, and his bomb was to "make enough noise to be heard above the clamor for war."

Muenter was captured after a failed attempt to kill J.P. Morgan, the New York financier, and took his own life while in jail.

This hardly stopped the bombs in the Capitol, however. In 1971, the Weather Underground planted a bomb in a Senate-side men's room of the Capitol to protest the U.S. bombing campaign in Laos, while in 1983, a group calling themselves the Armed Resistance Unit detonated a bomb to protest the recent invasion of Grenada. Neither of these two bombs injured anyone, though the latter did do great damage to a famous portrait of Daniel Webster.

No account of Senate scandals would be complete without mentioning at least some of the sex scandals that rocked the institution over the years. That senators were not immune to philandering had been clear at least since 1906, when Arthur Brown, who had been one of the first two senators from Utah ten years earlier, was shot by his mistress in a well-publicized affair. But nothing could compete with the news that a former president had fathered a child while still a senator.

The year was 1927. Warren Harding was long dead but far from forgotten. The fallout from his administration, most importantly the Teapot Dome

Senator Warren Harding, then presidential candidate, having a bust made of him by Helen Osborn. *Library of Congress.*

investigation, was still wending its way through the courts of the land. It appeared that his reputation could hardly fall any further when there appeared a book that outed Harding as a philanderer and one who had, in fact, fathered a daughter with a woman not his wife while he was a senator.

The book had the provocative title *The President's Daughter*, and it was written by one Nan Britton, a thirty-year-old woman from Harding's hometown of Marion, Ohio, and the mother of eight-year-old Elizabeth Ann, the daughter from the title of the book.

In its most famous passage, she describes an evening in January 1919 when she traveled down from New York City to visit Harding. She usually spent the afternoons alone, visiting some corner or other of D.C., but this afternoon, Harding had taken off, in spite of the busy schedule that the Senate had at the time.

> *That evening we went to his office in the Senate Building, which was then Room 314, later on he moved to Room 341, I think it was. I was in both offices I know.*
>
> *On our way to the Senate Office Building, we cut through the Capitol Grounds.*
>
> *"Some day you will be President" I said to him.*
>
> *"Say, you darling," he replied. "I've got the best job in the United States right now!" I think Mr. Harding did like being Senator…*
>
> *That particular afternoon and evening, however, he did spend with me up until ten-thirty or eleven o'clock. We went over to the Senate Office… We stayed quite a while there that evening, longer, he said, than was wise for us to do, because the rules governing guests in the Senate Offices were rather strict. It was here, we both decided afterward, that our baby daughter was conceived. Mr. Harding told me he liked to have me be with him in his office, for then the place held precious memories and he could visualize me there during the hours he worked alone.*
>
> *Mr. Harding was more or less careless of consequences, feeling sure he wasn't now going to become a father. "No such luck!" he said. But he was mistaken; and of course the Senate Offices do not provide preventative facilities for use in such emergencies.*

At first, the book did not appear to have much impact. In spite of the efforts made to keep it from being published, there was no real interest shown by the public in such prurience. This began to change after H.L. Mencken reviewed it in the *Baltimore Evening Sun*. Mencken chose not to dwell on "the tale of good Warren's mushy love-making" but, rather, found fascinating "the picture of him as statesman that emerges from the fair penitent's pages."

Whatever Mencken's purpose in reviewing the book, it soon began to sell extremely well. A further review from Dorothy Parker, which ran a few months later in the respectable pages of the *New Yorker*, described it as "lofty on the list of best sellers, despite the fact that it is allowed no advertising."

Parker also had no questions about its veracity: "Of the authenticity of Miss Britton's story I am absolutely convinced. I wish I were not. I wish I could feel that she had made it all up out of her head, for then I could give myself over to high ecstasies at the discovery of the great American satire, the shrewd and savage critique of Middle-Western love."

In spite of these two high-profile reviews, very little attention was paid to the book in the press of the day, and Nan Britton and her story were rarely mentioned—until 1931, when Britton sued Marion, Ohio innkeeper Charles A. Klunk for libel. She accused him of distributing the book *The Answer to the President's Daughter* by Joseph DeBarthe, which denied all the charges Britton had made in her book.

Unfortunately for Britton, she was unable to provide any concrete evidence of her long-running affair—and any papers that Harding had in his possession were either destroyed after his death or locked up in archives for decades to come—and she lost the case.

The actual truth of the matter has never been definitively proven one way or another. The discovery of letters Harding wrote to another woman, Carrie Phillips, proved without a doubt that Harding was a philanderer. However, as years pass, any chance of proving Elizabeth Ann's paternity becomes ever more unlikely. Even in the absence of proof, however, there is no doubt that Nan Britton's story will forever be part of the lore of the Senate.

Another story that is sure to live forever, and deservedly so, given its impact on a presidential race, is that of Gary Hart. In the spring of 1987, Gary Hart had everything going for him. He had finished out two terms in the Senate at the beginning of the year and was now running for president—and was the frontrunner for the Democratic nomination. He was also the subject of rumors of marital infidelity, though nobody had been able to prove anything thus far.

On Monday, April 27, reporter Tom Fiedler received a phone call at his desk at the *Miami Herald*. The caller told Fiedler that a woman who was Hart's mistress was going to take a flight from Miami to D.C. in order to meet Hart. Fiedler asked his colleague Jim McGee to check this out, and that Friday, McGee flew to D.C. With him on the plane was Donna Rice, a twenty-nine-year-old model/actress. After the plane landed, McGee was disappointed to see that Hart was not there to meet Rice, and in fact it was a woman who picked up his quarry.

Undeterred, McGee found out Hart's home address from a source on the Hill and went to stake out Hart's town house, half a block south of Marion Park and a little less than a mile southeast of the Capitol. He was rewarded that evening around 9:30 when Hart and Rice appeared from inside the house.

McGee called Fiedler, who took the first plane he could the next day to join in the investigation. On the way, he read a story in the next day's *New York Times Magazine*. Written by E.J. Dionne and entitled "Gary Hart: The Elusive Front-Runner," Dionne quoted Hart addressing the question of his womanizing: "Follow me around. I don't care. I'm serious. If anybody wants to put a tail on me, go ahead. They'd be very bored." This was all the impetus that Fiedler needed. After meeting with McGee and observing Hart and Rice on his own, as well as confronting Hart—who denied that Rice was staying with him—the two wrote an article that was published the next day.

Gary Hart's town house on Capitol Hill. *Photo by Otto Pohl.*

The day after the publication of the *Herald* story, Hart admitted that he had been on a ship named the *Monkey Business* with Rice. Unsurprisingly, the newspapers ran with this, and after four days of such headlines as "Hart's Campaign Reported in Peril Over Tryst Story"; "'I Have Not Slept With Gary Hart,' Rice Says"; and "Hart Admits `Mistake' but Denies Immorality," it was all over. One of Hart's campaign workers confirmed that Hart was, indeed, withdrawing.

Hart eventually re-joined the race, but his candidacy never caught fire, and after receiving only a few votes in the first primaries, he withdrew again in March 1988.

The most famous image of the whole affair was actually published almost a month after Hart's first withdrawal. On June 2, 1987, the *National Enquirer* published the famous picture of Rice sitting on Hart's lap on a dock. In the picture, Hart is wearing a T-shirt emblazoned with *"Monkey Business* Crew," referring to a luxury yacht belonging to a resort. This picture has become a true icon of senatorial scandal and has been parodied and reused endlessly since, ensuring that Hart and his peccadilloes will never be forgotten.

Chapter 4

The Navy Yard and Marine Barracks

Capitol Hill, in spite of its name, has always had two distinct centers of gravity: the aforementioned Capitol and then the Navy Yard/Marine Barracks area. Founded almost at the same time as the Capitol, both the Navy Yard and the Marine Barracks have a rich history of service and an exalted cast of characters who have served there. And, of course, a huge list of unsavory, corrupt and scandalous individuals.

The Navy Yard was founded a year before the federal government moved to its new home. It was the main center of shipbuilding for the United States Navy in its earliest years. The earliest scandal of the Navy Yard occurred when Commandant Thomas Tingey burned the place to the ground. Even more ironic was that Tingey had been the man most responsible for the building of the yard in the first place. In Tingey's defense, it must be stated that he was a) operating under orders from the secretary of the navy, and b) the British were riding into town, bent on its destruction—and might well have made good use of the ordnance stored at the Navy Yard for their own nefarious purposes. So while the British burned the Capitol and the White House, the navy burned its own shipyard. Fortunately, Commodore Tingey stuck around afterward to oversee the rebuilding of the yard.

The Marine Barracks were left unmolested during the British invasion, ostensibly due to the fierceness with which the marines had fought, thus earning the respect of their British opponents. The barracks are located just north of the Navy Yard, southeast of the Capitol, and were placed there by

Thomas Tingey's grave in Congressional Cemetery. *Photo by Otto Pohl.*

none other than Thomas Jefferson, who rode out with the commandant of the Marine Corps, William Ward Burroughs, to select the location.

Just over thirty years later, the Marine Barracks were shocked by the behavior of one of their own. In March 1838, Captain Augustus A. Nicholson had been nominated to be the second quartermaster of the Marine Corps. The first, Captain Elijah L. Weed, who had created the position and made it a permanent part of the corps four years prior, had died earlier that month, and the marines needed someone to take care of their supplies. Nicholson, born early in that century in South Carolina, had been orphaned as a boy, joined the marines as a midshipman and worked his way up through the ranks. Along the way, he had married Helen Bache Lispenard of a New York City family that had once owned considerable tracts of that city. Over the next seventeen years, even as Nicholson was posted all across the world, including the Mediterranean, they had eight children, of whom five survived—and another was born between Nicholson's getting the job as quartermaster and their finding a house.

It was clear that they needed a large house, both for their children and for the parties that they enjoyed throwing.

Fortunately, just such a property was available: the Maples. Built originally in 1795 by William Duncanson, it was one of the few grand houses on the Hill when Congress arrived in 1800 and had become one of the social

The Maples in 1936. After being sold by Major Nicholson, it was owned by Emily Edson Briggs (see Chapter 3). *Library of Congress.*

centers of the nascent city. Unfortunately, Duncanson was one of many to overestimate the potential of the city, and even before the federal government had arrived, he was broke. One of the trustees assigned to the case was none other than Francis Scott Key, at the time a little-known lawyer. Key ended up buying the Maples in 1815, and he repaired and expanded it.

The Maples was an ideal place for the Nicholsons. Blessed with enough space for both their children and their parties, it soon became, once again, a center of Capitol Hill society. In between the social whirl and the pressures of Nicholson's job, they managed to produce another two children, one of whom, Julia Barclay Nicholson, died in 1845. Around the time of the death of young Julia, Mrs. Nicholson began showing signs of strain. It would later be reported that she became subject to "sudden fits of insanity." Whether this was due to the death of her daughter, the strain of her eleventh pregnancy or the fact that she began to suspect her husband of cheating on her with Sally Carroll, daughter of Capitol Hill landowner Daniel Carroll, is entirely unclear.

In any case, on August 12, 1845, Virginia Bache Nicholson was born to Helen and Augustus Nicholson. This happy occurrence apparently did nothing to help poor Mrs. Nicholson. One month later, she went to visit her friends the Riells (or Riehls), who ran a boardinghouse at 3rd and Maryland Avenues. Mrs. Nicholson locked herself in a room, pushing out one of the Riell children who had followed her in. Another child then watched through the keyhole as Nicholson took a knife and, standing in front of a mirror, cut her own throat. The watching boy raised the alarm, and the door was broken down—but it was too late for Helen Nicholson, who bled to death before anyone could reach her.

The late Mrs. Nicholson was interred at Congressional Cemetery, and her unfaithful husband did not even wait a full six months before marrying again—to just that Sally Carroll with whom Mrs. Nicholson had suspected him of carrying on.

During the Civil War, the Marine Barracks and Navy Yard took on ever-greater importance. Though the commandant of the Navy Yard at the outbreak of the war, Franklin Buchanan, resigned his commission to

join the Confederacy, his replacement, John Adolphus Bernard Dahlgren, turned out to be more than able. Dahlgren had already lent his name to a new form of naval gun, the Dahlgren, which had been standard-issue for the navy for the past five years. Dahlgren was, unfortunately, only a lieutenant when Buchanan resigned and should have been at least a captain to take over the yard where he had been working for the past fourteen years. President Abraham Lincoln thus convinced Congress to pass a bill allowing this unorthodox move.

Lincoln turned out to be one of Dahlgren's biggest supporters and would visit

Portrait of Rear Admiral John A. Dahlgren. Taken in Mathew Brady's National Photographic Art Gallery during the Civil War. *Library of Congress.*

the Navy Yard whenever he could to see what was going on—and as a respite from the ordinary stresses of his job. This almost became his undoing in November 1862. Henry H. Atwater, the telegraph operator at the Navy Yard then, described what happened:

> *One evening a party of six or eight, including Mr. Lincoln, came to the Navy Yard and proceeded to the bulkhead, where they had arranged to demonstrate the workings of certain signalling [sic] rockets, several of which were sent up with good results. When the last one was tried each one in the party watched it as it soared aloft, leaving its streams of fire trailing behind, but when half-way up it exploded prematurely and fell to the water a miserable failure. "Well," remarked Lincoln, "small potatoes and few in a hill." I had never heard the expression before and it fastened itself in my mind.*

The expression that puzzled Atwater was actually an old saying from New England and means that something or someone is of no consequence.

Other observers maintain that some of the parts of the rocket came quite close to Lincoln and that he was indeed in far greater danger than he had let on. After all, not twenty years earlier, a similar accident had almost killed President Tyler.

The Navy Yard shortly after the Civil War. Docked is the USS *Polaris*, a Civil War–vintage tug later used for Arctic exploration, during which it reached the farthest north any ship had sailed at the time but was crushed by ice. *Library of Congress.*

The Navy Yard also had a small role to play in the Lincoln assassination. For one, the president stopped by the yard on the morning of his murder, and then later a number of the conspirators were held for several days on board the monitors USS *Saugus* and USS *Montauk*, which were moored just off the Yard. During this time, the body of John Wilkes Booth was examined on board the *Montauk*.

After the Civil War, the Navy Yard was used as a base for expeditions all around the world, including to the Arctic. It was because of this that it became involved in one of the more grisly stories related to Capitol Hill.

The Lady Franklin Bay expedition was set up as one of fourteen stations scattered around the globe, with twelve in the Arctic and two in the Antarctic, for scientific observation as part of the First International Polar Year. The principal research was to be done in meteorology and magnetism, in contrast to previous expeditions that had concerned themselves mainly with geography—and, in particular, the search for the Northwest Passage. In the end, thirteen countries manned the stations, making this a truly international effort.

The United States offered to man the station in Lady Franklin Bay, which is in the northeast corner of Ellesmere Island, just across the Nares Strait from Greenland. At eighty-one degrees north, it was the closest to a pole of any of the stations, and there was some talk of members of the expedition reaching the pole during their time in the Arctic.

The expedition was run by the U.S. Army, according to two acts of Congress that had passed in May 1880 and March 1881. The orders specified First Lieutenant Adolphus W. Greely as its leader, and he chose the other twenty-four members of the expedition. Most of them were drawn from the army, with only one sailor added, due to his experience as a mechanic: William H. Cross.

Cross had worked at the Navy Yard for many years and lived on Capitol Hill, at the corner of 2nd and D Streets SE, just up the street from Providence Hospital. He shared his house with his wife, Mary, their son and two sisters of his wife's, one an older widow whose daughter is also listed living with them and one younger, unmarried sister.

The expedition set out from St. John's, Newfoundland, on July 7, 1881, on board the *Proteus*. Stopping along the way in Greenland to pick up two final members of the expedition and send letters home, they reached Lady Franklin Bay by August 11.

At first, all seemed well. Mrs. Cross received two letters from her husband, one sent from Godhavn, Greenland, and delivered by a Danish boat, and

The SS *Proteus* in Lady Franklin Bay. *Library of Congress.*

the other from Lady Franklin Bay and returned to the United States via the *Proteus,* which had returned to St. John's after dropping off the expedition. His tone was cheerful, writing of the large number of animals that they had managed to shoot, the ease of the passage and—ominously, as it turned out—the lack of ice during the passage. In short, he was well pleased with how everything had gone thus far.

And then—nothing. Mrs. Cross was hardly surprised, as there was to be no contact with the expedition until the next year, when another ship was to go north and drop off supplies. Unfortunately, the *Neptune*, which was sent on this mission under the command of Sergeant William Beebe, turned back about 280 miles south of Greely and his men due to ice in the channel. On September 25, 1882, the *Evening Critic* reported this fact to the public, adding, "There will be no hope of reaching Lieutenant Greely before next summer."

The news the next year was no better. On September 13, the *Yantic* docked in St. John's and wired back to D.C. that it had not only failed in its mission to relieve Greely and his men, but that the *Proteus*—which had set out with the *Yantic* on this expedition—had been crushed by the ice during the mission, and its men had spent thirty-one days in the lifeboats before being rescued. It was now clear that the Greely mission was in great danger, but with winter closing in, there was nothing to do but to wait for the next summer. As the *National Republican* put it: "The prospects of the Greely colony encountering the rigors of a fourth winter beneath the Arctic circle are mournful to contemplate."

In 1884, a full-fledged expedition was mounted to rescue Greely and his men. Organized by William E. Chandler, secretary of the navy, and commanded by Commander Winfield Schley, four ships, including two from the British navy, were to ensure that the men would make it home safely.

The rough outline of the fate of the expedition, and the end of Mrs. Cross's uncertainty, was to come on July 17. As Mrs. Greely could read in the fifth paragraph of the late edition of that day's *Evening Critic*, her husband had passed away on January 1 of that year—a fact she was later to realize was incorrect. When Cross's remains were returned to her, she was told that he had not passed away until the eighteenth of January, just two days before his fortieth birthday. Another seventeen men had died between Cross's death and June 12, which was ten days before the camp was reached by Schley's boats. One additional member of the expedition died in Godhavn a few days later.

Over the next weeks, the newspapers reported the progress of Greely and his men, both living and dead, until on August 8, they arrived in New York. The bodies of the dead were brought to the hospital on Governor's Island, after which they were released for return to their families. William Cross's remains reached D.C. the next day and were taken to the Knights of Pythias hall on Pennsylvania Avenue SE.

On Sunday, August 10, an elaborate funeral was conducted for Cross. It began with a viewing at the house of the deceased, and the *Washington Post* calculated that over five thousand people were present. Mourners came to look at the "grim, iron casket that enclosed his remains" and extend their sympathies to his widow and son. The coffin, which had been made in St. John's, was "bolted and riveted" and thus remained firmly closed. The service, presided over by the Reverend Charles C. Andrews of Christ Church, included a ringing eulogy, in which Cross was described as "a hero in its best sense, because he was a stalwart, unflinching champion of duty." After the service, the crowd made its way down Pennsylvania Avenue and then to Congressional Cemetery, where the casket, "beautifully decorated with flowers," was placed in the public vault.

Two days later, the story of the Greely expedition, which had taken up large amounts of space in the newspapers, took a lurch toward the ghoulish. The *New York Times* reported that the navy was in possession of documents detailing "shocking stories of inhumanity and cannibalism": the desperate

William H. Cross's house on Capitol Hill. It is the dark house at the right. *Photo by Otto Pohl.*

men, with food running out, had been forced to eat the remains of their dead comrades. In fact, these stories had been known for three weeks, the *Times* alleged, but had been kept entirely quiet, with those few sailors from the relief expedition who were in the know sworn to silence.

The allegations, the *Times* continued, were the reason for the coffins used, stating that there was no need for such elaborate iron caskets—except to keep the corpses from being examined prior to interment. Commander Schley vigorously denied the charges, but subsequently, the coffin of Lieutenant Frederick Kislingbury was opened, and Kislingbury's body was found to have had most of the meat on his legs removed by a sharp instrument.

Mrs. Cross was asked whether she wished to have her husband removed from his coffin and have an autopsy done, but she demurred, stating that she would "prefer to remain ignorant." The matter was dropped, and it never came out what had happened to Cross after his death.

It was not the end of the story for the widow, however. Two years later, Greely himself published a book in which he described the expedition. His words regarding the late sergeant were hardly designed to give comfort to his widow.

Cross had soon been found out to be an alcoholic. He made some attempts to tame his inner demon and managed to celebrate his thirty-ninth birthday on January 20, 1883, in a sober manner, but thereafter, as the expedition became more trying, he began to backslide. He was suspected of imbibing of the fuel alcohol and used "mutinous, insubordinate, and disrespectful language." When found to be drunk on board one of the boats, he was removed from duty, but this hardly stopped his drinking. It had come as no surprise that he had died earlier than anyone else, with the cause of death almost certainly being alcohol.

Fortunately, the government of the United States had not entirely forgotten Mrs. Cross. On July 16, 1885, the *National Tribune* reported that Secretary of the Treasury Daniel Manning had offered her a post in his department, a job she held for many years.

Not all the scandals that rocked the navy and marines were of such a depressing nature. Some were, to be honest, fairly ludicrous, with the story of Francisco Fanciulli perhaps being the most extreme of its kind.

When John Philip Sousa left the United States Marine Band in 1892 to take up a position in Chicago, he left behind a great void. He had directed the group for twelve years and been a part of it since 1868, when he joined up at the tender age of thirteen. In the intervening years, he had made the band not only an integral part of the marines but also a nationally known ensemble. Finding the right man to continue his work was critical. It fell to Professor Francisco Fanciulli to take over the baton; he was given a five-year contract to do so.

Fanciulli, originally from Italy, had immigrated to the United States in 1876 at the age of twenty-three. He originally came over to be a private music teacher but had soon gone on to direct various orchestras and was thus well suited to replace Sousa.

For most of Fanciulli's term, all went well, with new marches being dedicated to him and an unbroken stream of marine band concerts taking place at the Marine Barracks. This all changed on Decoration Day 1897. Fanciulli and his band were to lead the marines from the barracks to the corner of 15th and Pennsylvania Avenues NW, from whence that day's parade was to start. Fanciulli had his band playing marches that were not suitable to the usual pace of the marines, so their leader, a Lieutenant Draper, sent a noncommissioned officer to the head of the band to request that the tempo be picked up.

Fanciulli refused, and so Draper himself approached him after they had arrived at their destination. Once again, Fanciulli refused, saying, "No, I prefer to select my own music." With this, Draper placed Fanciulli under arrest, which in this case meant that the bandleader had to spend the night within the confines of the Marine Barracks, rather than returning to his home in the neighborhood.

The lead cornetist took over the position at the front of the band, and the rest of the music played that day was, as Draper requested, "swinging."

Fanciulli was charged with insubordination and placed under arrest, though once again, this simply meant he could not leave the barracks, and in fact, he was treated as an honored guest. The actual trial did not take long, though the verdict was not publicized for a number of days. The *Washington Post* nonetheless had to fill the space allotted to the trial with some words and came up with this novel solution:

> [Francis H. Harrington, commanding officer,] *testified to the general character of the accused, and stated further that he had always found him most willing, courteous and obliging. So it is with Heurich's beer, it is courteous and obliging to the stomach and digestion. Had Lieuts Draper and Magill partaken of a cool and refreshing bottle of Heurich's beer before starting for the Memorial Day exercises, there would have been no complaint made of the music rendered.*

One hopes that Christian Heurich, D.C.'s beer baron, properly repaid this plug with a six-pack or two for the newspaperman who wrote it.

Once the guilty verdict had been rendered, it was passed on to the secretary of the navy, in this case Undersecretary Theodore Roosevelt. Roosevelt determined that the sentence of immediate discharge was too harsh and ordered him released from the barracks. It was rumored that Fanciulli would immediately request a discharge, but he completed the last couple of months of service before retiring in November 1897.

Fanciulli thereafter became the leader of the band of the Seventy-first Regiment of the New York National Guard and then later the Girls' Concert Band. He died in New York City in 1915, having never regained the fame he had known as leader of the "President's Own Band."

In the years following Fanciulli's retirement, both the Marine Barracks and the Navy Yard found themselves expanding rapidly, as the United States became more assertive in its intervention in foreign events and its foreign wars, whether the Spanish-American War or World Wars I and II.

The Navy Yard during the flood of 1936. *From the Historic American Buildings Survey. Library of Congress.*

The Navy Yard in particular spent these years as the U.S. Naval Gun Factory, as well as the testing facility. All this activity ensured a large number of sailors and marines in the area, and a booming industry grew around these two facilities to service their needs.

In 1951, Jack Lait and Lee Mortimer, two newspapermen, decided to expose the seamy underbelly of the nation's capital. Mortimer, known for his columns in which he wrote of night life as well as the doings of the criminal underworld, spent much of 1950 in Washington to find dirt. Lait, better known as an editor, worked for the *New York Mirror*, a tabloid that specialized in entertainment over news. The two were the perfect team for such an exposé.

Their book *Washington Confidential* was published in February 1951. It was long on innuendo and short on facts. As to the Capitol, they covered it in two sentences: "Many secretaries of Senators, Congressmen and executives are their office wives. All Congressmen's offices contain sofas paid for by the Treasury."

Much longer, however, is their report on the section of 8th Street SE that connects the Marine Barracks with the Navy Yard. First off, they declare it a "howling hell," a "skid row" to which no visitor, either local or out-of-town, would want to go. In fact, according to them, even the D.C. police force stayed away from the place, allowing, instead, the navy's shore patrol to do their work when fights broke out.

Lait and Mortimer save their greatest vitriol for the women of the strip, however, calling them "the frowsiest broads we have ever seen, dilapidated, toothless, drunk, swinging the shabby badge of their shoddy trade, long-looped handbags." Nonetheless, they felt it necessary to point out that the "worst and the cheapest" are to be found at the Ship's Cafe.

The *Washington Post* of this era presents a much different view of the area, with the main form of lawlessness being gambling, a charge that the muckrakers Lait and Mortimer entirely miss. And that the authorities are entirely oblivious to what is going on is countered by an article in the *Post* in which Guy Interdonato of Guy's Place (referred to as simply "Guy's" in the book) requests that the city keep the military from declaring his establishment off limits to servicemen. Furthermore, a few years later, the police have no trouble rousting a fifteen-year-old from the aforementioned Ship's Cafe on the charge of underage drinking.

The book was published to scathing reviews. Ben Bradlee, then a simple reporter for the *Post*, kicked off the counterattack with an article entitled "Even Addresses Are Wrong: Capital the Victim of Sloppy Reporting." His review starts by calling the book entirely useless, as "you can find out as much with a good 35-cent guide to Washington and a talkative taxi driver." It continues on with a list of errors found, from placing the Chinese embassy on completely the wrong street, to incorrect numbers of judges, to the ludicrous statement that the "Central Intelligence Agency is loaded with commies at the lower level" and, finally, the charge that they claimed to have "finagled" crime figures—which the FBI issues publicly. The article ends with the final slam, "Mistakes like that would cost a cub reporter his job."

Further reviews were equally vicious, but this was, in a sense, exactly what Lait and Mortimer had hoped for. In fact, it may have been part of the sales campaign of the book—on the inside flap of *Washington Confidential*, they proudly announced that their previous effort "was viciously attacked and vilified by public officials, notables and *literary critics* all over the country" (emphasis added).

Whatever their plan, it succeeded: the book became a bestseller. In contrast to Lait and Mortimer's previous books, *New York Confidential* and *Chicago Confidential*, no movie was made of this effort, and after publishing *U.S.A. Confidential* the following year, they got out of the dirt business entirely.

None of this should take away from the fact that this stretch of 8th was, indeed, not geared to the ordinary D.C. resident or visitor. With its tattoo parlors, drinking establishments and pawnbrokers' exchanges, it was truly geared to the sailors and marines who lived there.

One of the watering holes frequented by the marines was a restaurant by the name of Brinkley's. Founded in the 1930s by Jimmy Crandell, it began as a nightclub and restaurant. Brinkley's was a frequent fixture of the "What's Going On Around Town" columns of the local papers through the 1930s, but Crandell eventually sold out to two younger entrepreneurs, Theodore J. Scheve and William J. Schaefer. Under their guidance, Brinkley's began to garner slightly different news coverage, including being cited for serving underage drinkers, as well as running afoul of the Alcoholic Beverage Control Board for earning the majority of its income from alcohol rather than food. In short, it had become a dive bar and just the place for young marines to go to imbibe.

In 1999, Major Robert B. "Mo" Morrissey wrote of his memories of the place. It was the favorite place for one of his friends with whom he served at the Marine Barracks just after World War II. The two of them were assigned to the Marine Corps Institute (MCI), grading the efforts of marines stationed around the world who were working on a distance learning degree. In between their work in a rundown school nearby—this was before the MCI moved to the corner of 7th and G Streets—they were on funeral detail, marching through the extremes of D.C. weather to accompany soldiers to their final resting places.

Morrissey himself never went to Brinkley's, but his friend did, and Morrissey would be the one called by a sergeant who was moonlighting as a bouncer when his friend had, once again, overindulged.

Late one night, Morrisey was called out again and took charge of his very drunk comrade. As Morrissey heaved him across the street, his friend slurred at him, "You know, Mo, someday I'm gonna be a goddamned great actor." Morrissey, seeking to humor him—and get him out of the street—agreed. His friend did not hear the reply, as he had already passed out on the bricks that line the barracks.

The friend was none other than George C. Scott, and twenty years, four Oscar nominations and one win—which Scott declined—later, there was no doubt that he had, indeed, become a "goddamned great actor."

Chapter 5

The Scandals of J. Edgar Hoover

Few people have had their reputation decay as completely as J. Edgar Hoover. In life, he was the epitome of upright D.C., the G-man who always got his man, the confidant to nine presidents and, in short, a D.C. institution.

After his death, he has become, at best, a figure of derision. A closeted homosexual, possibly a cross-dresser, who managed to cling to power as long as he did through judicious use of dirt that he had dug up on both political opponents and allies. The revelations that came out after his death painted a picture entirely at odds with the image of rectitude Hoover had maintained throughout his life. Where did a man like this come from? How did he end up with two so completely opposite interpretations of his life?

Seward Square is the epitome of the infill development between the Navy Yard and the Capitol. Surrounded by houses built during the wave of construction that built up Capitol Hill around the turn of the twentieth century, it is a perfect place to live for those who work in and around the Capitol. Other than at rush hour, it is a quiet square surrounded by grand houses.

In one of these houses, on January 1, 1895, Anna Marie and Dickerson Naylor Hoover welcomed their fourth child. Their newborn was particularly welcome, as an older sister, Sadie Marguerite, had died a year and a half earlier, at not even three years old.

As a young boy, Hoover made a name for himself. This name was "Speed," either for the rapidity with which he spoke or for the eagerness with which he delivered groceries for vendors at Eastern Market. Hoover attended Central

High, where he was a member of the high school's regiment, as well as the debate team, and graduated as valedictorian, thus meeting Vice President Thomas Marshall, who spoke at the ceremony.

Hoover remained at home for college, attending George Washington University, where he was president of the Kappa Alpha Order. He received his undergraduate degree in law in 1916, followed by his LLM in 1917, earning money all the while working as an indexer at the Library of Congress, just a few blocks from his home.

Upon his graduation, Hoover was immediately hired by the Justice Department. Although he had been a member of the local militia and had registered on June 5 of that year—as every resident had to—Hoover's joining the Justice Department ensured that he would not be drafted, which was important to Hoover, as his father had to retire due to illness.

On November 19, 1917, Woodrow Wilson ordered the registration of all enemy aliens. A previous law, signed in April of that year, had already restricted the movement of all those who still possessed a passport from one of the nations the United States now found itself at war with. This new law required a new subsection of the Department of Justice to be formed, and the newly hired lawyer was placed in charge. Hoover took to his new job with relish, compiling a huge database of resident aliens in the country. It has been posited that his work at the Library of Congress gave him the tools needed to undertake this work, and that the cataloging of people was, to Hoover, the natural extension of the cataloging of facts.

At the end of the war, it took more than half a year for the new attorney general, A. Mitchell Palmer, to release those aliens who had been interned. Less than three months after Attorney General Palmer was sworn in, bombs planted in eight different cities exploded. One of the bombs was planted at Palmer's house in northwest D.C. There was an immediate push to boost the fight against radicalism. One step was to create an anti-radical division with Hoover in charge.

The first step Hoover took was to read the works of all the leading lights of Communist/anarchist bent: Marx, Engels, Lenin and Trotsky. He also began keeping files on everyone whom he suspected of any radical leanings, whether Communist, anarchist, anarcho-syndicalist or socialist. The anti-radical division, later renamed the General Intelligence Division (GID), went to work with a vengeance. Some three months after being formed, it was raiding the Union of Russian Workers, a group of anarchist Russian émigrés. A month later, Hoover was helping Assistant Attorney General Robert P. Stewart in the trial of some of those arrested, including famed anarchist Emma Goldman.

Aftermath of the bomb attack on Attorney General Mitchell Palmer's house. *Library of Congress.*

Shortly thereafter, Hoover stood on a dock in New York, watching the *Soviet Ark* cast off. The ship returned 249 people arrested during his raids, such as Goldman and fellow anarchist Alexander Berkman, to the Soviet Union.

It appeared to have been a full triumph for Hoover and Palmer, and the Palmer raids continued. In March of that year, however, Louis Freeland Post was made acting secretary of labor, and thus in charge of the Bureau of Immigrants, under which the deportations fell. Post asked for the records of those who had been arrested and discovered that many were unfairly in jail, such as some who had only been to a single meeting of a group deemed radical by Palmer and Hoover.

William Flynn, head of the Bureau of Investigation, tried to find dirt on Post, but there simply was nothing to be found, and eventually Palmer, Flynn and Hoover had to accept Post's decisions. In the end, almost three-quarters of the cases brought against arrestees were thrown out. Although a number of bombings continued for the next ten years or so, no further raids of the type that Palmer had organized were mounted again. Nonetheless, Hoover declared victory, writing that his arrests and deportations "had resulted in the wrecking of the communist party in this country."

The next year brought both triumph and sadness for Hoover. In March of that year, his father died and was buried in Congressional Cemetery.

Five months later, Hoover was named deputy director of the Bureau of Investigation. The new attorney general, Harry M. Daugherty, who had come in with the Harding administration, decided to bring in William J. Burns to head the bureau, and in keeping with the new broom sweeping clean philosophy, selected Hoover to assist him. In spite of his promotion, Hoover would not admit to working for the Department of Justice, as it was generally known as the "Department of Easy Virtue" at this time.

On August 2, 1923, President Warren G. Harding died. In the subsequent investigations into the excesses of his administration, questions began to arise regarding the decision to sell off the naval reserve of oil in the Teapot Dome. One senator from Montana in particular, named Thomas J. Walsh, was convinced that something had gone awry and that Attorney General Daugherty was somehow involved. He and his fellow Montana senator, Burton K. Wheeler, drove the investigation. Burns and Hoover were given orders to obstruct the investigation as much as possible by hiding evidence and subverting both senators. What, exactly, Hoover's role was in this is unclear, but modern researchers have concluded that Hoover "knew of, and may even have orchestrated, many of the illegal acts which had been used in the campaign to discredit" the senators.

Portrait of Thomas J. Walsh. *From the Harris and Ewing collection. Library of Congress.*

J. Edgar Hoover on December 22, 1924, the day he was made head of the Bureau of Investigation. He was not yet thirty years old. *From the National Photo Company Collection. Library of Congress.*

The whole edifice came crashing down in 1924. Daugherty was fired and, in the end, served time for his role, while Burns was removed as head of the Bureau of Investigation.

Hoover, in spite of his involvement, came out unscathed and, in fact, was made acting head of the bureau on May 10. Later that year, just ten days before he turned thirty, his job was made permanent.

The next eight years were relatively quiet for Hoover. The major source of criminal activity was Prohibition, and Hoover refused to get his agents involved in any anti-alcohol efforts, as he had seen the immediate effects on other police forces that had been forced to do so. Bootleggers found the policemen who were charged with enforcing Prohibition an easy target for corruption, and Hoover did not wish any stain to fall on his agents. He was well aware of the need for good public relations and ensuring that the name of the bureau was not dirtied.

Hoover's next great challenge came with the election of Franklin Delano Roosevelt in 1932. Roosevelt was sure to bring in a whole new team and, in particular, a new attorney general. Hoover's fears were fully justified when Roosevelt selected Thomas Walsh to lead the Justice

Department—the same Walsh whom Hoover and his team had thwarted eight years earlier. Newspapermen raced to the Caribbean, where Walsh was celebrating his recent nuptials to Mina Tiffin. When asked about his plans, Walsh replied that "he would reorganize the Department of Justice when he assumed office, probably with an almost completely new personnel." Others quoted him as saying that he would "kick that so-and-so John Edgar Hoover out of the window."

Either way, Hoover's days as bureau chief seemed numbered—until he received word that Walsh had died in the Pullman compartment that he and his wife were taking from Key West to Washington.

Hoover must have realized that this cast suspicions on him, so he was careful to send a bureau agent to help bring Walsh's body back to D.C. and then ensure that a medical examination of his remains was made, with full records kept thereof.

On March 5, 1933, Homer Stille Cummings was made attorney general. Hoover lobbied everyone he knew on Capitol Hill, whether they were involved in the process or not, to ensure that he kept his job. Neither Cummings, nor any other attorney general, ever made any attempts to oust Hoover.

J. Edgar Hoover fingerprints John Nance Gardner, Franklin Roosevelt's vice president, in this picture from circa 1939. *From the Harris and Ewing collection. Library of Congress.*

Hoover continued to make sure that the bureau received good press. The John Dillinger case is a good example. Hoover managed to involve the BOI in the search for Dillinger and his gang, in spite of the fact that the gang had thus far not broken any federal statutes and thus, did not fall under the purview of the BOI. Then twice, in March and April 1934, the bureau agents closed in on the man who was considered public enemy number one. Both times, in spite of the insistence—the second time by Hoover himself— that he was cornered and could not get away, Dillinger escaped. When the bank robber was finally killed after being ratted out by Anna Sage, Hoover turned this escapade into a great victory for the BOI, showing once and for all that his was the only police force that could protect the country effectively.

Another great public relations coup for Hoover was the movie *"G" Men*. Starring James Cagney, it showed the Federal Bureau of Investigation— it had taken on that name the same year the movie was released—at its finest, taking down all manner of bad guys. Hoover made sure that he watched it before it was released and gave his blessing. The FBI closely monitored the reactions to the movie, though there was no need for worry. The movie raised the profile and image of the FBI dramatically.

In spite of this, Hoover opened a file on Cagney and filled it with all kinds of rumors and anonymous denunciations. The file on him grew to well over three hundred pages, in spite of the fact that no charges were ever laid against him.

Cagney's was not the only file that Hoover kept on an innocent citizen. The biggest file—running to some three thousand pages—was kept on none other than First Lady Eleanor Roosevelt. It began when Roosevelt protested Hoover's investigation of two of her aides and grew from there, though much of it was simply the letters from outraged citizens concerned about her supposed un-American activities, for instance one in which the writer complained that the first lady had said, "Don't be afraid of radicalism." The letter writer, whose name has been redacted from the released FBI file, felt that this information must be passed on to the FBI immediately because "American men at this very time were being tortured and murdered by the world's no. 1 radicals!" Hoover wrote back, thanking the writer for their letter and enclosing a copy of a speech he had recently given, entitled "Our Duty to Youth." He did not add, as he had in another such letter, that the information given was "made a matter of permanent record in the files of this Bureau."

Other reports indicate a more targeted pursuit of the first lady, with long reports from special agents in charge from around the country added to the file, as well as articles written by or about Roosevelt. Many of the pages contain annotations by Hoover himself, including the tart note on the side of a 1951 *New York Times* article entitled "Mrs. Roosevelt Says M'Carthy is Menace." Roosevelt was quoted as saying, "He is the greatest menace to freedom because he smears people without the slightest regard for the facts. Mr. McCarthy has played on our fears. The people who follow him don't know that they are destroying our democracy." Hoover wrote, "She has done exactly this in her attacks on the FBI & when I called on her to produce fact she was unable to do so—H." Whether Hoover meant that Roosevelt had "played on our fears" or had accused the FBI of playing on them is unclear.

Hoover's world changed dramatically on February 22, 1938, when his mother died. She was buried in Congressional Cemetery next to her husband, and Hoover—who was still living on Capitol Hill—soon moved to upper northwest D.C., leaving behind—for the time being—the neighborhood in which he had grown up.

During World War II, the FBI claimed a great victory over German spies when it arrested eight men who had infiltrated the country with hopes of sabotaging the American war effort. After the arrests were made, Hoover was happy to accept the profuse thanks of the citizens whom he had saved. However, it was, once again, simply a happy accident that these spies had been captured: one of their number, George John Dasch, had become disillusioned with Nazi Germany and had gone to the FBI to turn himself in. In spite of the manhunt that was going on, it took Dasch's tossing of $84,000 on the desk of an FBI agent to convince him that he was, indeed, one of the wanted men.

Six of the spies were put to death in the electric chair in the district jail, far out on Capitol Hill. Dasch and Ernest Peter Burger, who had helped turn in the others, were sentenced to long stretches in prison, though these sentences were commuted after the war.

After the war, Hoover's interest returned to his old favorite: Communism. With the rising strength of the Soviet Union, he found many willing fellow anti-Communists in the government, the chief of whom was Senator Joseph McCarthy. Hoover also instituted a program whereby the FBI was responsible for checking the background of government workers, a program that helped him almost double the size of the bureau over the next six years.

With this newly strengthened organization, Hoover was able to help McCarthy in his work to discredit people all through the government, including Secretary of State Dean Acheson. McCarthy exploded into the national spotlight with a speech to the Republican Women's Club of Wheeling, West Virginia. It was during this speech that he held up a sheet of paper, claiming that it contained a list of members of the Communist Party who were also

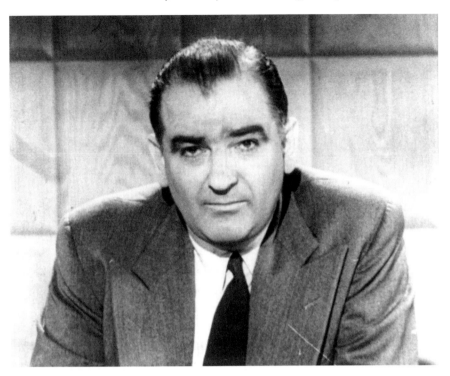

Senator Joseph McCarthy in 1954, the year of the Army-McCarthy hearings. *Library of Congress.*

working at the State Department. Though the number of names on the list remains in dispute—McCarthy never gave the list to anyone—the names and information that McCarthy used had come from Hoover and his investigations into the backgrounds of government employees.

For the next four years, McCarthyism held sway over Washington. From his post as chairman of the Senate Committee on Government Operations, McCarthy sent out subpoenas to all those whose loyalty to the United States he questioned. McCarthy's witch hunt resulted in the famous Army-McCarthy hearings, during which the conflicting accusations that these two had traded over the previous year would be sorted out. For three months, the two teams slugged it out in the Senate Caucus Room of the Senate office building, culminating with Joseph Welch's heartfelt plea to McCarthy, in regards to a young lawyer working with Welch: "Let us not assassinate this lad further, Senator; you've done enough. Have you no sense of decency, sir? At long last, have you left no sense of decency?"

Hoover wisely kept in the background during this tense time, knowing full well that it could backfire on him as it had on McCarthy. Hoover did, however, support McCarthy in public. In 1953, when the FBI was already investigating McCarthy, Hoover was asked about the senator. Hoover answered that in his opinion, McCarthy was "earnest and honest."

This brief quote caught the eye of a reader in Larchmont, New York, who sent a letter to Hoover requesting the full speech from which this was taken—as well as a list of any Communist agents that McCarthy had managed to uncover. Hoover's reply was short to the point of rudeness, writing that his comments were "given orally to a reporter" and that "the statement speaks for itself." Hoover entirely ignored the second request.

In short, Hoover's connection to McCarthy was both important and well hidden. In Ellen Schrecker's 1998 book *Many Are the Crimes*, she states that the FBI was "the single most important component of the anti-communist crusade," adding: "Had observers known in the 1950s what they have learned since the 1970s, when the Freedom of Information Act opened the Bureau's files, 'McCarthyism' would probably be called 'Hooverism.'"

Thus, even after McCarthy's downfall and eventual retirement from the Senate, Hoover kept up the fight against Communism, with all the methods at his disposal. Hoover enlarged and improved surveillance of those he felt were somehow related to Communism but went much further, actually running operations against those he feared.

One of the earliest attempts in this direction was Hoover's use of his agents in smearing Adlai Stevenson, then running for president. Hoover wanted to ensure that Eisenhower and Nixon were elected and would stop at nothing to gain this end. His agents were thus instructed to loudly speak of Stevenson's sexual orientation over lunch, knowing full well that there were many ears open at the Mayflower Hotel dining room that would be more than happy to pass on this information. How much this whisper campaign actually changed events is impossible to determine, though it is extremely unlikely that it changed the outcome of what was, indeed, an extremely lopsided election.

In the 1950s, Hoover institutionalized his methods by creating COINTELPRO (Counter-Intelligence Program). As succinctly summed up in a Senate report in 1976, its purpose was "protecting national security, preventing violence, and maintaining the existing social and political order by 'disrupting' and 'neutralizing' groups and individuals perceived as threats." Unfortunately, the disruption soon devolved into increasingly elaborate operations against citizens, organizations and even members of Congress.

One of these was Adam Clayton Powell Jr., representative from Harlem, who made his home in Gessford Court, a small Capitol Hill alley one mile east of the Capitol. Powell bought a number of the houses in the 1950s, fixed them up and sold some of them, while keeping number 16 to live in and number 18 to rent out. Powell lived in this small house while Congress was in session, alone for the most part. On weekends and during spring break, his son, Adam Clayton Powell III, would come to visit, occasionally helping out in his father's office.

In those months when Congress was in session, a steady stream of illustrious visitors made their way gingerly down the alley, looking for the house with the Jaguar parked out front, to have a quiet talk with the representative. Famous names included Hubert Humphrey and Barry Goldwater. Visitors were received in the small living room, where the furniture consisted of three chairs and a couple of TV tables. Such cramped quarters were a small price to pay for the opportunity for a quiet chat with the powerful head of the Education and Labor Committee, meetings that were unlikely to be noticed by the press: the only reporters who made their way to Gessford were those working for the African American press.

One day, Powell and his son came home during the day unexpectedly, and Powell's son noticed something amiss with the rear window of their house. He thought there was a bird sitting in front of it, but his father explained that the window was actually broken. As they pulled in front of the house, they saw someone make his escape around the back of the alley. Inside, nothing had been taken, though papers had been disturbed, and there was glass on the representative's bed in the back bedroom. Powell immediately realized that this was no ordinary burglary and suspected that it had been performed at J. Edgar Hoover's behest.

When Powell called the head of the FBI to ask what that was all about, Hoover claimed that those who had broken in were acting on some threat or another. Powell accepted the FBI chief's explanation but asked that in the future, they make use of the key hidden under the doormat to spare him the expense of a new window and the trouble of cleaning glass shards off of his bed.

While this particular instance of a "black bag operation"—a warrantless search—was fairly harmless, the damage done by COINTELPRO over the years was almost impossible to assess. The number of people falsely accused, incarcerated or simply gunned down is long and probably will never be determined with complete accuracy.

The program continued until March 8, 1971, when a group calling themselves the Citizens' Committee to Investigate the FBI broke into a field office in Pennsylvania. The information they found there was published in newspapers across the country, and readers found themselves confronted with an entirely different face of the FBI than that which Hoover had so carefully nurtured over the past forty-five years. Hoover thereafter swore that he had reformed his—and the FBI's—ways, and the public moved on to other matters, including, a year later, the greatest scandal of the twentieth century, the only one to bring down a sitting president, the scandal that will always be tagged with the name of the hotel in which it occurred: Watergate.

Although there are no reasons to believe that Hoover had anything to do with this scandal—in fact, Hoover was under far too much fire from the COINTELPRO revelations to help Nixon—it is speculated that Nixon had his own incompetent team attempt the break-in after Hoover refused to help.

J. Edgar Hoover died on May 2, 1972. His obituary in the *Washington Post* the next day was mainly positive, though it does quote Dr. Benjamin Spock, who had been prosecuted for his anti-war work, as saying, "It's a great relief." Hoover was given the great honor of lying in state in the Capitol Rotunda.

After Hoover's funeral, his body was taken to Congressional Cemetery, where it was laid to rest next to his parents and sister. Even as preparations were being made for Hoover's funeral, his legacy was being questioned. In an article published the same day as his obituary, Jack Anderson wrote,

J. Edgar Hoover's grave in Congressional Cemetery. In the same plot are his parents, Dickerson and Annie Hoover, and his sister Sadie Marguerite. *Photo by Otto Pohl.*

"The FBI has been guilty of excesses. These abuses of power should occupy President Nixon in his search for Hoover's successor."

Though there had been many rumors about Hoover before his death, they became a veritable flood thereafter. Using the powers of the relatively new Freedom of Information Act, journalists and authors began reading through old FBI files and discovering for themselves the breadth of Hoover's work. Above all, people were intrigued with Hoover's sexuality. Here was a man who had been married but had also spent most of his time—both on and off the job—with another man, Associate Director of the FBI Clyde Tolson.

Tolson had been a low-level FBI agent with only three years on the job when he was selected to be Hoover's right-hand man. The two men were thereafter inseparable, working closely together, eating their lunch at the Mayflower Hotel every day, taking vacations together and, although they maintained separate residences, often sharing their evening meals. Hoover's driver would pick up Hoover and then Tolson every morning, and Hoover ate dinner with Tolson the night before he died.

The thought that the man who had spent so much of his career using sexual deviation as a cudgel with which to smear his enemies was himself gay was too delicious to pass up, and a whole cottage industry grew up around finding dirt on Hoover, the more salacious the better.

A row of graves at Congressional Cemetery. Clyde Tolson's grave is in the foreground, sixth from the end. Hoover's grave is on the right side, with the bench in front of it. *Photo by Otto Pohl.*

The most lasting image of this man is that of a cross-dresser. In his 1993 biography of Hoover, Anthony Summers claims that Hoover was observed multiple times in women's clothing. His source for this, however, was Susan Rosenstiel, who was notorious for her lies. With no further evidence, and with Hoover's well-known reticence, there is no reason to believe that there is any truth to the rumor—but in popular culture, the image of the strait-laced and image-conscious FBI head as a cross-dresser lives on.

Far more important to his ultimate legacy are the papers that have been released from the FBI files, which show the real J. Edgar Hoover and his ruthless and paranoid style of running the country's police force.

For now, however, there are still plenty of people, particularly FBI agents both current and former, who are willing to stand up for Hoover's reputation. They still make the pilgrimage to Congressional Cemetery where J. Edgar Hoover found his final resting place, just a mile from where he was born. He lies only a few spaces away from where Clyde Tolson was buried a few years later.

Chapter 6

Burying the Scandals

Congressional Cemetery has been an important part of Capitol Hill history from the day it opened, and the roster of representatives and other Hill worthies who are buried there is long and illustrious. Fortunately for this tale, there are also many buried there whose moral rectitude was less than perfect.

To begin with, the whole cemetery was placed in a way incompatible with the original plan of D.C. The 1791 L'Enfant plan clearly states, "No burying grounds will be admitted within the limits of the City, an appropriation being intended for that purpose without." This was, as so many other aspects of L'Enfant's plan, completely ignored: by 1798, there were two squares within the city designated for burial. The square in the northeast quadrant of the city, responsible for the interment of all who died in the eastern half of the city, was inadequate due to it being located on swampy ground. Thus a group of citizens banded together to ensure that those east of the Capitol would also have an appropriate place to bury their dead. They chose square 1115, which is between E, G, 18th and 19th Streets, for a cemetery.

Although there were nominally a private group of people, most were members of Christ Church, Capitol Hill's oldest church, located on G Street between 6th and 7th Streets, a little over a mile due west of the planned cemetery.

On April 4, 1807, the cemetery committee registered their subscription as "Washington Parish Burial Ground." In spite of the private manner in which it was started, they always planned on turning it over to Christ Church to actually run it, although it was meant for the whole community.

The grave of Senator Uriah Tracy, on right. Beneath the cenotaph is the brick mausoleum in which the senator is actually buried. *Photo by Otto Pohl.*

The land was bought on April 15 from the city; there were stipulations on the sale ensuring that everyone, even the poor, could be buried there. In less than five years, the sale of plots had covered the cost of the land, and it was turned over to Christ Church.

The first burial happened four days before it was officially bought. The buried man was William Swinton, a stonecutter who had been hired by Benjamin Latrobe, superintendent of construction of the Capitol.

The first congressman to be buried there was Senator Uriah Tracy of Connecticut, who died July 19, 1807. He was not the first congressman to die in D.C., though the exact number and whereabouts of the previous remains are unknown. History records Tracy as having been a pretty much scandal-free representative, with his closest brush coming in 1803 when he proposed having New England secede from the Union—in spite of serving as a senator at the time. He died after catching some illness while attending the funeral of one Abraham Baldwin, senator from Georgia, at Rock Creek Cemetery.

After Tracy's burial, the new cemetery—referred to simply as the "Burial Ground in the Eastern Branch"—became the principal resting place for those congressmen who died in office. Although the families of the deceased generally would have preferred to bring their remains home, the state of the roads—and the lack of refrigeration or any other means of keeping the body from decaying before being interred—made a local burial de rigueur.

With the cemetery's new role as resting place for deceased congressmen, it was decided that each one deserved more than a simple headstone. Benjamin Latrobe, taking time out from his duties of making the Capitol a reality, was asked to design a fitting memorial. Latrobe set to work and came up with something that could not possibly be mistaken for any other tombstone. It consisted of a large square block, set on a slightly larger base and surmounted by a conical top. On the inset sides of the block are inscribed the name, office and age of the man buried beneath.

In contrast to other Latrobe creations, this one did not meet with universal approval. One of the earliest criticisms came from Frances Trollope.

Trollope is best known as the mother of English novelist Anthony Trollope but was also a well-known writer in her own right. In 1832, after having spent several years in the United States, she published a book entitled *Domestic Manners of the Americans*, and in it she describes a funeral of a member of Congress.

While generally quite taken with the "ceremony and dignity" of the occasion, and particularly by the number and rank of the dignitaries who participated, she was less than impressed with the grave markers she saw: "I did not see the monument erected on this occasion, but I presume it was in the same style as several others I had remarked in the same burying ground, inscribed to the memory of members who had died at Washington. These were square blocks of masonry, without any pretensions to splendour."

A few years later, her criticism was echoed by George Watterston, third librarian of Congress. In his book *A Picture of Washington*, he describes the cenotaphs as "very plain and rather tasteless." The most strident denunciation of Latrobe's creation, however, came from Massachusetts representative George Frisbie Hoar.

In 1876, a bill that would end the custom of adding a monument to each member of Congress who died in office was wending its way through Congress. Since many years had passed at this time without any congressman choosing to be actually buried at Congressional Cemetery, it seemed that there was also no need to keep honoring all those who were buried elsewhere. One of the provisions in the act indicated that any further cenotaphs should be built to match the previous ones. This roused Hoar to proclaim the following:

> *It is certainly adding new terrors to death to propose that in any contingency, whatever may be the poverty or degradation of any Member of Congress,*

his body should be put under a structure similar to the cenotaphs now there, which are only excusable on the ground that nobody is buried under them. I can not conceive of an uglier shape to be made out of granite or marble than those cenotaphs now there. To propose gravely to require by law that for all time structures of that fashion shall be placed over deceased Congressmen seems to me a little too bad.

Since then, only a couple of cenotaphs have been added and only under special circumstances, and most do not follow Latrobe's ill-chosen design.

It was not just members of Congress who were interred here, however. In 1812, Vice President George Clinton died in office. He was interred in Congressional Cemetery, though almost a hundred years later, he was moved to Kingston, New York, near his birthplace. Clinton, who had also been the first governor of New York, lived a blameless life, making him totally unsuited

to this tome. Fortunately, two years later, another sitting vice president died and was buried in Congressional Cemetery. This was Elbridge Gerry, and his is a name that will live forever, though probably not for the reasons Mr. Gerry would have hoped.

In 1812, Gerry was governor of Massachusetts as a member of the Democratic-Republican Party. His party redistricted the state, putting the heavily Federalist Party areas into one district, and thus ensuring that all the others leaned Democratic-Republican. A cartoonist for the *Boston Gazette*, looking at the shape of the new Federalist-dominated district, felt that it most closely resembled a salamander and drew a cartoon with this shape, naming it the "Gerry-mander."

The grave of Elbridge Gerry. *Photo by Otto Pohl.*

"The Gerry-mander: A New Species of Monster, Which Appeared in Essex South District in January Last."

The *Boston Repertory and General Advertiser* took an even harder line, stating, "The district may well be exhibited as a *Monster*. It is the offspring of moral and political depravity. It was created to drown the real voice of the majority of the citizens of the county of Essex."

Gerry lost his election for governor—freeing him up to run for vice president—but his name has remained ever after affixed to the practice his fellow politicians had created in redrawing districts for partisan benefit. Over the years, the hyphen has disappeared, but the practice of gerrymandering remains alive and well to this day.

Congressional Cemetery even played an admittedly small part in the Lincoln assassination conspiracy. Lewis Powell, along with David Herold,

David Herold photographed at the Navy Yard by Alexander Gardner in April 1865. *Library of Congress.*

was given the task of assassinating Secretary of State William Seward. After their attack failed, both fled, with Herold meeting ringleader John Wilkes Booth in Maryland. Powell, for his part, became disoriented and eventually fell from his horse. It is said that he spent three very cold nights in Congressional Cemetery before being caught after he returned to Mary Surratt's boardinghouse.

Herold and Booth were both chased down in Virginia, and while Booth was killed, Herold was captured and, along with Powell, tried and convicted. Both were hanged, along with two other conspirators, on July 7, 1865, at the Washington Arsenal. They were all buried there.

Three and a half years later, Herold's mother and sisters were given permission to exhume his body and have it reburied in Congressional Cemetery, next to his father, who had died in 1864.

The grave of Beau Hickman (foreground). *Photo by Otto Pohl.*

Herold was far from the only inhabitant of Congressional Cemetery with a somewhat checkered past. The saga of Robert Hickman and the route he took to his final resting place is certainly instructive. Hickman, who was generally known as "Beau," was your classic man-about-town. Born about 1810 near Richmond, Virginia, into a wealthy family, Hickman inherited a sum thought to be about $40,000 (about $800,000 in 2010 currency) on his father's death. Sadly, his extravagant lifestyle left him broke after just a couple of years. He requested more money from his brother-in-law, William Eaton. Eaton acquiesced and handed over $10,000, but with the caveat that he never see Hickman again. With this money, he moved to the nation's capital and began a life that became notorious throughout D.C. The *New York Times*, in its obituary, described him thus: "Beau concluded that the world owed him a living. Too proud to work, too honest to steal, he adopted a vagabond, Bohemian life, and, levying a tax on all who came in contact with him, made it pay."

Hickman, who himself never gambled, was known as someone who knew horses and would freely give advice—expecting five or ten dollars in return. Although he was extremely well dressed when he arrived in D.C., his clothes soon began to suffer as his money ran out. His favorite dodge to remedy this situation was to go to a tailor, have a new suit made and then, when the bill was presented, claim that "his friend, President Jackson, who was a d—d good fellow, no matter what some folks might say, had borrowed a thousand dollars of him and it was really impossible just then." The tailors, impressed by the names being dropped, would assume that Hickman was good for the newly tailored clothes, and by the time they realized Hickman's true financial situation, it would be too late to demand the clothing back.

Hickman employed similar ruses in dealing with hotels and managed to live for quite some time in the best addresses in the city, all without ever paying anything for the pleasure. Hickman never drank, though he did enjoy a cigar now and then, and when given money for drink, he would either use it to pay for his dinner or to buy a cigar. He would also earn money by leading visitors around the city, interspersing his commentary with stories of the presidents and congressmen whom he had known throughout his career.

Unsurprisingly, this lifestyle was not sustainable, and sometime just before the Civil War, he began to go downhill. The first sign of this came in 1860, when Hickman was arrested in New York for attempting to scam a resident. Prior to this incident, Hickman had been known for his punctiliousness in his dealings—except with tailors and innkeepers. Shortly thereafter, his clothes became shabby, and he took on the stumbling gait of a rheumatic. He did, for a while, wear a quite remarkable suit made of velvet and covered in tiny bells, which he would shake to signal his presence when entering any establishment.

Hickman spent the last years of his life almost destitute, and so it came as no surprise to anyone when he was taken from his humble rooms on Maryland Avenue SW to Providence Hospital in late August 1873. He died on September 1 and was quickly buried the next day in the potter's field near the Washington Asylum.

A day later, a group of his friends took up a collection to give Hickman a proper burial. With the money in hand and an undertaker hired for the job, they went to the intendant of the asylum, who showed them to the grave, which was found to have been robbed, leaving only his torso behind. His arms and legs had been cut off, and though the face remained, the skull had been removed. Even the torso was not undisturbed, as it had been cracked open and the heart—which was found a few feet away, wrapped in newspaper—removed.

A new coffin was procured, and what remained of Beau Hickman was transferred to Congressional Cemetery, where he was given a proper burial that was well attended. His death was broadcast far and wide, with multiple New York City papers honoring him with lengthy obituaries.

Congressional Cemetery was also the target of several grave robbers—or resurrectionists, as they styled themselves. Though never legal nor a proper trade, grave robbing had a long history, as the need for cadavers for medical schools was great and the number available through such sources as executed criminals was small.

Though some medical students took matters into their own hands, most of the time they hired out the job to professionals. There were quite a number of these who plied their trade in D.C., including William Jansen, Maud and Percy Brown, William Beall and George A. Christian.

William Jansen was the most famous of the lot. He styled himself the "Resurrectionist King" when he went on stage to describe his work. Jansen, who was said to have been born in Denmark, worked all the way up and down the East Coast of the United States and spent a fair bit of time in the nation's capital. His arrival would be heralded by articles in the local papers, and Jansen gladly gave them material by spending his time twitting the local police by planting stories that he would steal a corpse for the local police chief. Jensen even went so far as to show, on stage, how he went about his work. Unfortunately for those who paid to watch this, they were treated first to Jansen mumbling inaudibly on the stage, then taking a drink to fortify himself and finally staging a resurrection during which the "corpse" displayed a dismaying ticklishness that left both him and the audience laughing. Finally, Jansen, who had retreated into the wings of the stage, reappeared and said, "Now you have seen all about it, and I don't see any necessity for more talk."

When not speaking with newspapermen or mumbling at audiences, Jansen stole a fair number of bodies, including at Congressional Cemetery. A story he told after being arrested by D.C. police for the crime of having stolen a body in Baltimore concerned the aftermath of an expedition to this cemetery. As Jansen told it, a storm commenced just as they were completing their gruesome task, and so they fled to the nearest shelter—which was the local jail. Riding out the storm under the portico of this edifice, the night watchman came out to see what was going on. Jansen asked him whether the watchman knew him. The watchman purportedly replied, "Yes, you are Burgdorf [another noted grave robber] and I don't desire any closer acquaintance with you."

"Then you can mind your own business," rejoined Jansen, which the watchman indeed did, leaving Jansen to finish up his gruesome expedition once the storm slackened.

George A. Christian better fit the image of a body snatcher. Ostensibly a clerk in the surgeon general's office, he supplemented his meager income with stints as a resurrectionist. After he was caught in 1873 with a body he had taken from a cemetery in western D.C., a perusal of his diary indicated that he had been up to his tricks at Congressional Cemetery as well. Noted within was that he had been responsible for resurrecting the body of one A.C.H. Webster, a well-to-do claim agent who had died the previous year. A further entry suggested that Christian and his gang were responsible for the outrage perpetrated on Beau Hickman's body the previous year.

Christian was sentenced to jail but was out again by the end of the next year—and up to his old tricks. Now sporting a "Dr." in front of his name, he was living out on the eastern edge of town.

That he was again engaged in his former trade came to light when a police officer investigated two mysterious boxes that had been dropped off at the Baltimore and Ohio railway depot and discovered that they contained two bodies, one of which was still "limber and warm."

Finding the two men who had dropped off the box proved to be an easy matter, and they led officers to a house at 1327 East Capitol Street, where Christian was found, along with Percy and Maud Brown.

At this point, life seems to have gotten too hot for Christian. He was next sighted in New York, involved in a further famous grave robbery there, as well as being linked with an attempt to steal Abraham Lincoln's corpse. He died a few years later in Philadelphia. His dying wish was to be left to lie until his body had decayed enough to be of no interest to a resurrectionist.

Percy and Maud Brown proved to be a remarkable pair. Maud, in particular, made extravagant claims as to her heritage, insisting that she was a noble born in Russia who had been forced to go to the Crimea to help translate during the Crimean War and had lost most of her sight because of this.

She eventually made her way to the United States, collecting Percy—who might have been her brother or her husband, no one was ever sure—along the way. She was originally listed as an abortionist, though later the pair seems to have given themselves over entirely to grave robbing. Maud Brown was particularly adept at this game. She would attend funerals as a mourner and then leave some indication of which grave had recently been filled.

Maud and Percy Brown stayed in D.C., though their situation rapidly devolved over the years. While in 1888 they were living in a "cave" below a house at the corner of 3rd and Massachusetts Avenues NE, they were reduced to living in the most straitened circumstances in a building called, presumably ironically, Ryder's Castle. Although once indeed a fine mansion, it had fallen into considerable disrepair and was inhabited—though not owned—by one George Ryder. A 1895 *Washington Times* article entitled "Hymns Mingle with

Orgies" gave the whole unpleasant story of a tumbledown house that was filled with the marginalized of society.

Despite the fact that the Browns had turned their backs on grave robbing, instances of this practice continued to appear in the news. A particularly sad occurrence transpired at Congressional Cemetery in 1889. On December 14 of that year, Alvina Cheek, only twenty-four years old, died of tuberculosis at her home on Capitol Hill, leaving behind her grieving husband, Thomas. They had been married all of two and a half years. Her young child died at about the same time, and three days later, after a funeral at her home, she and her child were interred in Congressional Cemetery.

Three days after that, William T. Clinton was patrolling what was then a desolate stretch of Capitol Hill near 17th and A Streets. While on his patrol, he noticed a horse-drawn carriage draw near. Knowing that this quiet area was often the scene of the crime for resurrectionists, he concealed himself and, when the carriage drew near, jumped out and caught the horse's reins. When the driver realized that any attempt to flee with the horse was futile, he jumped and ran, as did his two guards, who had been walking fore and aft of the carriage. While Clinton struggled with the horse, the three made good their escape.

Once he had the horse under control, it took but a moment for Clinton to uncover the freshly unearthed bodies that lay under the cover on the back of the carriage. Clinton took his prize to the morgue, where the bodies were taken into custody. The next day, newspaper articles described the horse and carriage in great detail, and it was not long before someone claiming to be the owner thereof, Arthur C. Adams, a local doctor, stepped forward. It took longer to determine the identity of one of the dead women, who was described as "a refined woman."

Fortunately, the robbers had not stripped the body of her garments— something they were wont to do because there was no law against stealing bodies, but taking their garments was clearly theft—and they revealed the words "B. Cheek."

It was not long before Thomas Cheek had confirmed to the police that this was, indeed, the woman he had buried only a few days earlier. The only question that remained was who, in fact, had stolen the body—and how they had managed to do so without disturbing the grave site. Adams stoutly maintained that he had no part in this and that the horse and buggy did not belong to him. In fact, he appeared to have a cast-iron alibi, having been at the medical college at the time. Questioned as to why he had claimed the team, he replied that he was just doing his friend Dr. Beall a favor: "If I had known that there was going to be so much do about it, I would never have troubled myself about the case."

A warrant was thus sworn for the arrest of Dr. William W. Beall, a sometime barber and dentist. Beall was found just after Christmas, tried, found guilty and sentenced to six months in jail. Beall managed to gain a new trial, in which the jury was hung—and he was found loitering around another cemetery later that year.

About ten years later, Congress finally acted to put a brake on these occurrences and passed "An Act for the promotion of anatomical science and to prevent the desecration of graves in the District of Columbia." In the intervening years, however, grave robbing had already become a rare event and one whose every occurrence caused the newspapers of the time to reminisce about the bad old days of Jansen, Christian and the Brown siblings.

This is not to say that grave robbing disappeared entirely. In fact, well over one hundred years after poor Mrs. Cheek's indignities, Congressional Cemetery was once again the victim of the attentions of a resurrectionist. In this case, the perpetrators were not after anatomical specimens but rather were looking for body parts for their own nefarious purposes. On June 4, 1991, two area residents were arrested and charged with stealing from churches. Around the same time, bones believed to be from Congressional Cemetery were discovered, though it was unclear whether these two occurrences were related. In any case, the caretaker of the cemetery took the opportunity to check up on all the graves—and discovered that the White family vault had been opened and ransacked.

William Wirt, in an engraving by Charles Fevret de Saint-Mémin from 1807 or 1808. *Library of Congress.*

William G.W. White was an early investor in Washington, D.C., having bought and built on numerous lots. He, like so many others, did not do as well as he had hoped and was eventually hauled in front of the Supreme Court to sort out his troubled finances. White eventually retired to

Philadelphia but did not forget his adopted town and elected to be buried there. Over the years, almost two dozen of his relatives were added to the vault, as well.

An even stranger loss of remains came to light about twelve years after the White case. One day in late 2003, the manager of the cemetery received a mysterious phone call from someone claiming to have William Wirt's skull. Wirt had been the U.S. attorney general from 1817 until 1829 and had run for president in 1832. Fortunately, he did not win, as he was to die less than a year after he would have been sworn in. Since 1834, Wirt—and presumably his skull—had been lying in the Wirt vault of Congressional Cemetery.

The caller added that the skull had been stolen in the mid-1980s and had ended up in the collection of an eccentric individual, who wished to remain anonymous for obvious reasons. The manager tried to convince the caller to identify himself, or at least return the skull, but he rang off.

Instead, a few months later, another call came, this time from a much more public figure: D.C. council member Jim Graham. Graham explained that he had now taken possession of the skull and wished to return it.

In the end, it took a year to effect this return, partly because the vault was no longer locked but instead was closed via a large stone, making the entry—and thus the determination that it really was Wirt's skull—that much more difficult, and partly because the remains inside had been strewn around so vigorously that determining which bones belonged to which of its inhabitants was almost impossible.

Fortunately, D.C. is the sort of city where experts in all manner of esoteric subjects are to be found, and so the crew from Congressional Cemetery was soon in touch with Douglas Owsley, a forensic anthropologist at the Smithsonian. Owsley was able to match the skull—which had come in a box marked "Hon. Wm. Wirt"—with the bones. Wirt's skeleton once again now rests, almost complete, in his vault.

Mary Ann Hall lies beneath one of the most elaborate headstones in the cemetery. Atop a tall stone pedestal sits a woman, thinking, one hand at her cheek, the other on her knee, holding a wreath. What the sculptor—or the person who chose the sculpture—wanted to express with this is unclear. Certainly, it gives no hint as to Hall's life. If anything, it is an attempt to celebrate her generosity and the many people she helped in her life. It makes no mention of what Hall's job was or how she earned her money.

Hall left behind very little of a personal nature. No photos exist of her, she wrote no diary, no tell-all book, and she did not keep a little black

The grave of Mary Ann Hall, on right. Buried with her is her sister Elizabeth. The grave to the left contains another sister of Hall's, Catharine, as well as their mother, also named Elizabeth. *Photo by Otto Pohl.*

book, something that certainly came as a great relief to those who availed themselves of her service.

Mary Ann Hall was, not to put too fine a point on it, a madam. For many years around the Civil War, she ran one of the best—and presumably most profitable—brothels in D.C. It was located just below the Capitol, on the 300 block of Maryland Avenue SW. This proximity to the Capitol ensured a steady stream of well-heeled clients, in spite of the generally insalubrious nature of the neighborhood, situated as it was on a canal.

When the Smithsonian began its work on the National Museum of the American Indian, it found a huge trove of interesting—and revealing—artifacts. The garbage dump used by Hall's establishment revealed gilt-edged porcelain, a plethora of champagne corks, wires and seals and the remains of a remarkable variety of food including coconut and turtle.

Hall first appears in D.C. in the 1840 census, sharing her house with four other unmarried women as well as two slaves. There is no doubt that she prospered over the next twenty years, with the value of her property increasing dramatically from one census to the next. In contrast to the other establishments of her type across the city, she had very little contact with the authorities, and in fact, when a fellow brothel-keeper was in court in 1863, the lawyer complained that his client was constantly being harassed, while the likes of Hall were left untouched.

Possibly piqued by this, the authorities did take a closer look at her operation, and in early 1864, Hall was indeed arrested, charged and convicted of "keeping a bawdy house." In spite of this slight setback, Hall continued to prosper, and the whole Civil War came as an enormous boon to all levels of prostitutes in the district.

Hall operated her establishment until the early 1870s, when she turned over its day-to-day operation to one Elizabeth Peterson, who is listed in the 1880 census simply as "Prostitute." A few years after that, however, Hall's house at 349 Maryland Avenue was being used as a dispensary. Hall herself was living on her savings and helping out her friends where she could.

The November 14, 1881 edition of the *Washington Evening Critic* tells a heartrending story of Mary Ann Hall's generous nature. It seems that a "notorious character" by the name of Jenny Davis (or McCann) had died two days earlier after dosing herself with laudanum. The coroner's jury seems to have had no trouble with declaring this a suicide, though Davis had complained about stomach cramps earlier that day and was intoxicated at the time. She died penniless, and so Mary Ann Hall, who is noted to have "lived with the deceased" and "kept a house of ill-fame in this city," indicating to the discerning reader what, exactly, had been the nature of Davis's notoriety, helped to buy her a plot in Congressional Cemetery and a funeral as well. Cemetery records indicate that, indeed, a "Jennie Davis" was interred on November 15, 1881.

Five years later, it was Hall's turn. On January 29, 1886, at the age of seventy-one, she succumbed to a cerebral hemorrhage and was buried three days later. Prior to her death, she had been, once again, living at her house on Maryland Avenue. The *Evening Star* had only a few words to say on her passing, but they were heartfelt: "With integrity unquestioned, a heart ever open to appeals of distress, a charity that was boundless, she is gone but her memory will be kept green by many who knew her sterling worth."

Mary Ann Hall today lies surrounded by her mother and two sisters in a large, well-kept plot.

Chapter 7

Almshouses, Workhouses and Jails

L ooming over the gravestones of Congressional Cemetery is a large brick building with surprisingly small windows: the D.C. jail. It was placed there for the same reason that the cemetery originally was, namely to be as far from the population centers of the city as possible. Making this an even easier decision was the fact that the land around there, ominously named Reservation 13, belonged to the federal government and was thus free to be used as a dumping ground for all sorts of unsavory buildings, including the jail, the crematorium, the workhouse and the poorhouse. All of these have added their stories to the history of Capitol Hill.

The Washington Asylum, as it was then called, was the first to be built, in 1839. A large brick building, it was built across from the intersection of C and 19th Streets SE. The asylum was a combination workhouse, where those who had run afoul of the laws of the District of Columbia were housed, and poorhouse, a place of last resort for the city's indigent, with the two different areas separated by a thin wooden wall. For the first thirty-five years, this building quietly went about its business—with the added job of taking in any animals found running at large after 1853—appearing in the pages of the local newspapers only when more money was requested for its operation. The only time it made news that traveled outside of the city was when an inmate made an escape attempt and was killed by one of the wardens.

The open area around the asylum was also perfect for a graveyard, and a potter's field was laid out for use by the indigent D.C. citizens. The asylum was responsible for the building of the rough wooden coffins used in the burials there.

The north wing of the D.C. jail. *Photo by Otto Pohl.*

During the Civil War, the quiet was occasionally interrupted by grand reviews of the Union army; the area around the almshouse remained overwhelmingly empty and thus furnished the space necessary for such a large operation. The Civil War also brought more inmates to the asylum when a number of men cracked under the strain of waiting for the expedition to begin. But mainly, the asylum and workhouse continued their quiet existence, ignored by the vast majority of citizens of D.C.

This all changed in 1873 when the recession now generally referred to as the Long Depression began and thereby dramatically increased the number of people seeking shelter in the asylum. On December 1, 1874, William Birney, assistant attorney of the District of Columbia, wrote his report to the D.C. commissioners, in which he requested a number of changes to the laws governing the asylum.

Included within this report was the impossible overcrowding of the asylum, along with the plea that the workhouse and the poorhouse be separated: "The pauper and the criminal are crowded together. This is probably the only place in the United States where poverty and crime are placed by statute on the same level, and it is to be hoped that the discreditable exception will be made to disappear at once."

Three years later, the *National Republican* filed an even more damning report. A reporter, having read a report to the grand jury in which the inmates were described as "huddled in one loathsome filthy mass of rats, vermin and dirt," sensed a story and went to see for himself. His front-page exposé showed the state of the workhouse to be even worse than he had imagined: "The small room was jammed with a reeking mass of degraded wretches, shouting, singing ribald songs, and it seemed to the startled reporter that he had caught a glimpse of Hades itself. His heart was sickened by seeing here and there a youthful innocent face peering curiously out from that breeding school of iniquity." In contrast, the almshouse next door "was found to be clean and comfortable," and the almshouse's hospital was also fairly acceptable, "although the buildings are nothing but frame shanties."

Fortunately, the district commissioners heard the outrage and had a new workhouse built. It was a good-sized building farther south of the almshouse, at the northeast corner of E and 19th Streets. Some twenty years later, the *Washington Times* paid a visit and published a full-page, mainly positive, story about the workhouse. The inmates were crowded into their rooms, with twelve to fifteen men obliged to share, but at least they had "wholesome, well-cooked food, even if it does not come up to the menus of the city restaurants and the grand hotels" to look forward to. The men were put to work on chain gangs, with some sent across town to Rock Creek Park, while others stayed closer to home, regrading 18th Street, just a few blocks from their erstwhile home. As punishment, there was only the "glad room," an otherwise empty room with a window to the outside. "No man has been known to remain more than twenty-four hours in the glad room."

The article includes the hopeful statement that a new building was soon to open, which would reduce the overcrowding somewhat. In short, it was as upbeat a story as could be hoped for such a place.

Even more optimistic was a story published, again by the *Washington Times*, in late 1906. Here, the object of its inquiries was the women's workhouse. Housed in an old, Civil War–era powder magazine located southeast of the men's house, the staff, and particularly the prisoner's aid society, were praised for their ability to rehabilitate the unfortunates who had been sent here.

That same year had also seen major changes in the almshouse. The general feeling was that having the almshouse and jail in such close proximity unjustly painted the residents of the former with the sins of the inmates of the latter. A strip of land along the Potomac just south of its confluence with the Anacostia was selected, and new houses were built there. On September 25, 1906, the *Washington Post* proudly announced that the almshouse's charges were in the process of being moved to the new location, with "many pathetic and humorous incidents" marking their move.

How the Workhouse In Washington Sometimes Makes Good Women Out of Bad.

SUFFERING

Illustration showing the D.C. Women's Workhouse. From the *Washington Times*, December 23, 1906. *Library of Congress.*

As to those left behind, matters came to a head in 1908. In particular, the conditions of the jail were of concern, but the Senate, and in particular Senator Jacob Harold Gallinger of New Hampshire, wanted a report on all of the buildings that had grown up on Reservation 13 over the years. An appropriation was made, a three-man commission was selected and on December 31, 1908, they delivered "The Report of the Commissioners appointed to investigate the jail, workhouse, etc., in the District of Columbia."

The report mainly echoed what the *Times* had found five years earlier, though it found the workhouse to be "crowded far beyond its normal capacity," and it was thus "not possible to give adequate employment to the great majority of those confined."

The commission spent a fair bit of ink trying to decipher the mass of often-conflicting laws and jurisdictions that regulated which prisoners were held where for which crimes. In the end, its recommendation was to close everything and start over elsewhere. This path forward was accepted, and in 1910, the Occoquan complex opened, with the first inmates being those of the workhouse.

With the overcrowding issue solved—at least temporarily—it came time to address one final problem. The almshouse had not only held the poor and indigent but also soon evolved into a hospital of last resort. Over the years, particularly during the various epidemics that washed through the city, small wooden shacks were added around the main house in order to take in those suffering from disease. While the initial intent was good, the almshouse was chronically under-financed, and the frame shanties were hardly up to their task. By 1900, there was no doubt that something had to be done, as there was no space left for patients, and one of the dining rooms had been converted into a ward. The crowding also prevented effective separation of sick patients, forcing tubercular patients into wards with patients suffering from other diseases. Even after the other facilities were moved, or improved, the hospital remained, occasionally berated for some minor misdemeanor or other but mainly ignored, and it a took truly horrifying story published in the *Washington Times* on March 12, 1916, to make any changes.

The article was entitled "Occoquan a Paradise Compared with Refuge of Cut's Ill and Needy" and started off with the simple statement, "Washington cares for its lawbreakers better than it looks after its indigent sick." In contrast to the Occoquan workhouse, where an inmate could look forward to living in a "bright, healthful dormitory," a patient at Washington Asylum Hospital was taken to a "ramshackle firetrap of a wooden-walled ward." The buildings were "gloomy and crowded; the atmosphere is bad. There is no ventilation." A patient had to hope to be amongst the truly sick, as then there was a chance that he would be in the actual ward and not a basement or "a bleak, windswept, unsheltered porch."

Having gone through a number of further generalities, the article went on to the specifics, in the form of the actual article written by the investigator, Mary Noyes Whiteford. Her article started off with a bang: the asylum hospital was "the most disgraceful public building in the Nation's Capital." She pointed out that numerous government buildings had been built recently—but no money was ever available for the hospital. Warming up to her theme, she continued with a description of one of the wards and its contents. The beds "are almost as old and rickety as the building. The ventilation in this building was vile. In fact, there was no ventilation to speak of." The food also came in for its share of scorn. Cooked in another building, there was no real way of reheating it in the ward, and it was served lukewarm at best. After this, however, her story degenerated into a listing of the people who were receiving care there and their often-tragic stories.

Whether because of this story or other similar ones, the city finally did do something about the situation, opening Gallinger Municipal Hospital in 1922. It would be renamed D.C. General Hospital in 1953 and serve the D.C. community until 2001.

Today, the only one of these facilities that remains on Reservation 13 is the D.C. jail. Originally located in northwestern D.C., it was moved to the corner of 19th and B Streets—as Independence Avenue was called at the time—in 1875, with great hopes that it would prove to be a more humane place than the "Blue Jug," D.C.'s infamous first jail, that it replaced.

The district jail circa 1909. Photograph by Barnett McFee Clinedinst. *Library of Congress.*

The jail became nationally famous as the place where Charles Guiteau, who shot President Garfield, was incarcerated. On September 11, 1881, ten weeks after the assassination attempt and a week before the president succumbed to his wounds, Guiteau himself was the object of gunfire: Sergeant John A. Mason, a Union army veteran, shot through a window into the cell occupied by Guiteau. Mason, who was stationed at Washington Barracks and had been ordered to stand guard at the jail, was court-martialed and sentenced to eight years in prison.

In the meantime, Guiteau's trial had come to its foregone conclusion, and he was sentenced to die. The public followed the steps taken closely, with the major newspapers of the day filling their entire front pages with detail-filled accounts of Guiteau's last few moments on earth.

The jail once again vanished from public memory for the next twelve years, until its condition became too deplorable to ignore. As so many times before, the problem was simple overcrowding, and it would take many years for anything to be done in this regard. Eventually, prisoners were farmed out to other institutions, including Occoquan, but the old jail remained in use, despite a regular drumbeat of articles attesting to its unacceptable conditions. The jail achieved some notoriety during the Second World War when the German spies in the Dasch ring were executed there.

Finally, almost one hundred years after it was built, the city decided it was time to act. In June 1971, the building of two new jails was announced, with one being placed near the current jail and the other nearer the courts themselves. Unfortunately, it would take another four years for ground to

Cartoon from front cover of *Puck* magazine, showing Charles Guiteau as a crazed office-seeker. Cartoon by "WAT." Originally published July 13, 1881, while President Garfield was still alive. *Library of Congress.*

be broken, during which time the ACLU would come out with a report denouncing the jail as a "filthy example of man's inhumanity to man." The *Washington Post* summed up the report as speaking of "brutality by guards, insanitary living conditions, lack of proper medical care, overcrowding, idleness and infestation by rats and roaches." On October 2, 1972, eight prisoners escaped from this hell, climbing through the attic of the ancient building and fleeing down a fire hose and over the fence.

It should not have come as too great a surprise that emotions would eventually boil over.

Early in the morning of October 11, 1972, a group of inmates took control of one of the cellblocks of the jail. They took eleven guards hostage and demanded to see both Kenneth L. Hardy, the head of the D.C. Corrections Department, and William L. Claiborne, a *Washington Post* reporter who had done much to publicize the atrocious conditions within the jail.

Claiborne was brought into Cellblock 1, which his colleague from the *Post* described as such: "The atmosphere inside the cellblock was oppressive: the single bulbs covered by wire mesh at intervals in the ceiling gave off little light. In the early hours before dawn, the cellblock was cold and dank. A strong smell of urine permeated the entire cellblock."

After an initial round of discussions, Claiborne was released to act as a go-between, while Hardy was kept as a twelfth hostage. Their demand was simple: freedom—in the form of $1 million and a jet plane—or death. Their grievances were similar to others across the country, but they had a particular grudge against Hardy, whom they felt had dealt more honestly with the demands made at the Occoquan penitentiary than their own.

Only about fifty prisoners were part of the takeover, as others in Cellblock 1 asked to be put in other parts of the prison. Their request was granted. There followed a long, tense standoff, with the prisoners occasionally appearing, usually with Hardy, and shouting additional demands.

Numerous politicians, including then–school board member Marion Barry, attempted to negotiate. Late in the afternoon, there was a breakthrough when six inmates plus a number of negotiators, including Hardy, were taken before a judge so that they could state their case. With the assurance that they could continue to address a judge and that they would not receive any further reprisals due to their actions, the prisoners then released their hostages around 12:30 a.m. In spite of the guarantees previously given, fourteen of the prisoners received extra sentences, ranging from one to ten years.

Shortly after this, the jail found itself in charge of some famous inmates: a number of the Watergate conspirators, including G. Gordon Liddy and

Howard Hunt. Liddy ended up spending a fair bit of time there after being arrested for his part in the coverup, including eight months spent in the D.C. jail after refusing to testify.

Even as he was serving his time, a new jail was being built. On September 12, 1973, there was a groundbreaking ceremony for a new facility. It opened on March 29, 1976—and was immediately deemed too small for the 1,200 inmates of D.C., meaning that at least one of the cellblocks from the old jail continued to be used.

Remarkably, there was a jail on Capitol Hill even earlier than any of these. It was not originally built as such—in fact, it had been built almost fifty years earlier as a temporary structure—but was pressed into service during the Civil War.

On August 24, 1814, the British burned the Capitol, as well as a good portion of the rest of Washington, D.C. This led to calls for the capital to be moved farther inland—Cincinnati was suggested—but a group of landowners, worried that the value of their property in the federal city would drop precipitously if that came to pass, chipped in to build a temporary Capitol across the street from the burned building.

The temporary Capitol was used from December 15, 1815, until 1819, during which time James Madison was inaugurated on its steps. With the Capitol rebuilt, Congress moved back into its original digs, and the threat of moving the capital was banished. The temporary Capitol thereafter became first a private school and later a boardinghouse much used by congressmen. Eventually, the rooming house closed, and the building remained unused until the outbreak of the Civil War, at which point it became a federal jail.

As a federal prison, it was used to house prisoners considered a threat to the country: traitors, prisoners of war and, above all, spies. Why keeping Confederate spies and other such people across the street from the seat of government seemed a good idea at the time remains uncertain. Maybe it had something to do with "keeping your friends close and your enemies closer." Some of the famous inmates at the time were the Confederate spies Rose O'Neal Greenhow and Belle Boyd and the Confederate raider John Mosby.

Rose O'Neal Greenhow, who had enabled General P.G.T. Beauregard to win the Battle of Bull Run, was caught by Allan Pinkerton when he observed her receiving information from a Union soldier. After being held under house arrest for few months, she was transferred to the Old Capitol Prison, along with her eight-year-old daughter, Rose. She was taken to a room that was "furnished in the rudest manner—a straw bed, with a pair of newly-made

Rose O'Neal Greenhow and her daughter "Little" Rose, in the Old Capitol Jail. Photo by Mathew Brady. *Library of Congress.*

unwashed cotton sheets—a small feather pillow, dingy and dirty enough to have formed part of the furniture of the Mayflower," as well as a few sticks of furniture. Greenhow spent about four months in the jail, during which she managed to continue to send messages to the Confederate army—all the while complaining about her treatment at the hands of the Union—or Abolition, as she preferred to refer to it—army.

Belle Boyd, who had smuggled information to General Thomas "Stonewall" Jackson, enabling him to beat General Nathaniel Banks in the Shenandoah Valley, was caught after she gave a letter to General Jackson to

The Henry Wirz execution in the Old Capitol Jail. *Library of Congress.*

a man whom she believed to be a Confederate but was actually a Unionist. Her review of her time in the Old Capitol Prison is much less negative than Greenhow's; in fact, she lists the remarkable—though monotonous—menu served here every night. Boyd only spent a month in the jail before being repatriated as part of a prisoner exchange at Fortress Monroe.

John Mosby's stay at the prison was even shorter than Boyd's. He had been on his way to visit his wife when he was captured at the train depot by Union cavalry. He was taken to Washington and jailed in the Old Capitol but was released ten days later. Presumably, his captors had yet to appreciate his talents that he would put to such good use over the next few years.

Most of the prisoners were not as well known but had been captured either smuggling goods into the Confederacy or attempting to break the naval blockade. In fact, not even all were Confederates: some were Union soldiers who were being court-martialed.

The building was used as a prison for a while after the war, holding a number of the Lincoln conspirators, including Dr. Samuel Mudd and Mary Surratt. It was during this time that one of its most macabre moments came.

On November 10, 1865, Henry Wirz, the commander of the Andersonville prison camp, in which almost thirteen thousand Union soldiers died, was executed on the grounds of the Old Capitol Jail, in sight of the Capitol.

Thereafter, the temporary Capitol went into a serious decline, and by 1867, a visitor to the city complained that it was being used as a henhouse. Shortly thereafter, the building was sold, and after a number of different uses including the headquarters of the National Women's Party, it was torn down to make room for the Supreme Court in 1935, replacing the brick structure with one of the many marble-clad edifices that inhabit Washington, D.C.

A Guide to the Misdeeds

K een-eyed readers may have noted that there are no scandals written up that have happened since 1987. This should not be construed as meaning that Capitol Hill politicians and residents have suddenly avoided scandalous behavior or become more adept at hiding their misdeeds.

Quite the contrary. The intervening years have made for rich pickings to the student of scandal, and new technologies have made for new ways of embarrassing yourself before your peers. However, if tragedy plus time is comedy, as Carol Burnett once said, so scandal plus time equals entertainment. Those recent scandals have not yet matured enough to become worth including in a book such as this.

For those who are interested, a brief glance at any newspaper will give more than enough fodder for any student of modern scandal. And, in time, today's scandals will be added to the canon of Capitol Hill stories, as well.

In the meantime, rest assured that as long as there are people living and working on Capitol Hill, there will be no shortage of new scandals, either.

This book had its genesis in a walking tour developed by Tim Krepp and the author, covering the scandals of Capitol Hill. In this spirit, there follows a list of locations that can be viewed when visiting Capitol Hill. The sites have been clustered by location for ease in finding them, rather than by subject matter.

The Capitol

The Capitol is visible from most parts of D.C. and is open for touring six days a week. Go to www.visitthecapitol.gov to book a tour. [Chapters 1–3]

Elizabeth Ray's office was in 1506 Longworth Office Building, corner of Independence Avenue and South Capitol Street SE. [Chapter 1]

Warren Harding's office was in room 143 of the Russell Senate Office Building. [Chapter 3]

The *Senate Caucus Room* is on the third floor of the Russell Senate Office building, which is at the corner of Constitution Avenue and 1st Street NE. [Chapter 5]

The *Library of Congress* is at 101 Independence Avenue SE. [Chapter 5]

Old Capitol Prison was at the corner of East Capitol and 1st Streets NE. Today, this is the site of the Supreme Court Building. [Chapter 7]

Seward Square

J. Edgar Hoover's birthplace was at 413 Seward Square SE. Although long gone, the house was located where the overhang to the right of the United Methodist Church now stands. [Chapter 5]

The *Jenrette House* is at 160 North Carolina Avenue SE. [Chapter 1]

Gary Hart's town house can be seen at 517 6th Street SE. [Chapter 3]

The Maples is located at 619 D Street SE. It is also visible from the 600 block of South Carolina Avenue. [Chapter 4]

Providence Hospital has moved to northeast D.C. Its former location is now Providence Park at 2nd and D Streets SE. [Chapter 2]

William H. Cross's house is at 324 2nd Street SE. [Chapter 4]

Eastern Market

Eastern Market is at 225 7th Street SE. [Chapter 5]

Florence Kubel lived at 1000 East Capitol Street NE. [Chapter 1]

Laura L. Dodge lived at 651 A Street NE. [Chapter 2]

Gessford Court is between Independence Avenue, C, 11th and 12th Streets SE. There are entrances on 11th and 12th Streets, midway down the block. [Chapter 5]

MARINE BARRACKS/NAVY YARD

The *Marine Barracks* are at 8th and I Streets SE. They can be toured every Wednesday at 10:00 a.m. More information at www.marines.mil/unit/barracks/pages/welcome.aspx [Chapter 4]

The Navy Yard's main entrance is at M and 6th Streets SE. www.history.navy.mil/branches/org8-1.htm

Guy's Place was located at 531 8th Street SE. [Chapter 4]

Brinkley's Restaurant was at 533 8th Street SE. [Chapter 4]

David Herold's house was on the east side of 8th Street SE between L and M Streets. It is a gray house with a green roof. [Chapter 6]

CONGRESSIONAL CEMETERY

Congressional Cemetery's main entrance is at 18th and E Streets SE. More information about the cemetery and its tours is to be found at congressionalcemetery.org. [Chapter 6]

Christ Church is at 620 G Street SE. [Chapter 6]

The *Old D.C. Jail* was located at the corner of 19th Street and Independence Avenue. Today the St. Coletta School occupies the space. [Chapter 7]

The *D.C. Almshouse* was directly across from C Street at 19th Street. [Chapters 6, 7]

Men's Workhouse was located on the NE corner of 19th and E Streets SE. Today, this is home to part of the D.C. jail. [Chapter 7]

Women's Workhouse was due east of Congressional Cemetery, where the rest of the D.C. jail stands. [Chapter 7]

ELSEWHERE IN D.C.

The *Patent Office* is now the American Art Museum/National Portrait Gallery at 8th and F Streets NW. [Chapter 2]

The *Baltimore and Potomac Station* is no more; it is once again part of the Mall. It was located at 6th Street and Constitution Avenue. [Chapters 2, 7]

Mary Ann Hall's brothel was at 349 Maryland Avenue SW. The house is long gone, and the site is now used by National Museum of the American Indian. [Chapter 6]

The *Mayflower Hotel* still operates at 1127 Connecticut Avenue NW. [Chapter 5]

Bibliography

INTRODUCTION

"L'Enfant's Reports to President Washington, Bearing Dates of March 26, June 22, and August 19, 1791" *Records of the Columbia Historical Society*, vol. 2: 1899.

CHAPTER 1

Battiata, Mary. "The Congresswives Strike Back!: Rita Jenrette, Sit Dawn, Hush Up and Listen Here!" *Washington Post*, 4 Mar. 1981: B1.

Bruskin, Robert. "'Kick-Back' by Romney's Aides Told." *Washington Post*, 14 May 1947: 1.

Caplan, Stephen P. "J. Parnell Thomas Dies." *Washington Post*, 20 Nov. 1970: C12.

Clark, Marion, and Rudy Maxa. "Closed-Session Romance on the Hill: Rep. Wayne Hays' $14,000-a-Year Clerk Says She's His Mistress." *Washington Post*, 23 May 1976: A1.

Dickens, Charles. *American Notes for General Circulation.* London: Chapman and Hall, 1842.

Dutkin, Howard. "'New Low in Politics,' Thomas Calls Clark's Payroll Probe." *Washington Post*, 24 Oct. 1948: M1.

Forbes, Edgar Allen. "Famous American Duels: The Cilley-Graves Duel." *New York Tribune Sunday Magazine*, 6 Dec. 1914: 10.

Hazelton, George Cochrane. *The National Capitol: Its Architecture, Art and History.* New York: J.F. Taylor & Company, 1914.

Jenrette, Rita, and Kathleen Maxa. "Diary of a Mad Congresswife: Thoughts and Observations Most Political Wives Only Share Among Themselves." *Washington Post Magazine*, 7 Dec. 1980: 8.

———. "The Liberation of a Congressional Wife." *Playboy*, Apr. 1981: 199.

Jones, George, and E.M. Boyle. "Jonathan Cilley of Maine and William J. Graves of Kentucky, Representatives in Congress: An Historical Duel, 1838: As Narrated by Gen. Geo. W. Jones, Cilley's Second, to E.M. Boyle, in Philadelphia Press." *The Maine Historical and Genealogical Recorder* 6 (1889): 385–95.

Latham, Aaron. "How the Washington Post Got the Goods on Wayne Hays." *New York Magazine*, 21 Jun. 1976: 33.

Lyons, Richard L., and Mary Russell. "Wayne Hays Reported Ready to Step Down." *Washington Post*, 1 Sep. 1976: A1.

Medford (OR) Mail Tribune. "Political Fakir, Street Masher and Cheap Liar." 9 August 1911: 4.

National Tribune (Washington, D.C.). "A Public Thief and Great Scoundrel." 12 Dec. 1889.

New York Herald. "Silcott Found: The Treasurer Who Decamped with $98,000 Belonging to Our Congressmen Discovered in Terrebonne, Canada." 31 Jan. 1890.

New York Times. "Congressmen in Poverty: Plight in Which Silcott Left Them." 7 Dec. 1889.

———. "Silcott's Capture Reported." 1 Mar. 1890.

Pearson, Drew. "New Thomas Charges Are Aired." *Washington Post*, 17 Sep. 1948: C11.

———. "Thomas Held Ignoring Old Adage." *Washington Post*, 4 Aug. 1948: B13.

Ray, Elizabeth L. *The Washington Fringe Benefit.* New York: Dell, 1976.

Roberts, Roxanne, and Amy Argentsinger. "Rita Jenrette's New Take on an Old Sex Scandal: That Night on the Capitol Steps." *Washington Post*, 29 Nov. 2011.

Stokes, Dillard. "Confession of Farnsworth Tells How He Sold U.S. Secrets to Japanese Attaches Here: Story Reveals Theft of Bomb Sight Plans." *Washington Post*, 23 Jan. 1940: 1.

Washington Post. "House Office Shortage Set at $112,000." 6 Jan. 1947: 1.

————. "Recent Bride and Charming Addition to Young Matrons of Naval Society." 6 Feb. 191: ES7.

Washington Times. "Eastern High School Girls Who Take Prominent Part in Irish Fairy Play Tonight for School Art Fund." 6 May 1911: 7.

————. "Rep. Lafferty Was Impressed by Newspaper Photograph." 7 Aug. 1911: 1.

United States. Cong. House. *Being the Second Session of the Sixth Congress: Begun and Held at the City of Washington, November 17, 1800, and in the Twenty-Fifth Year of the Independence of the Said States.* Washington, D.C.: Gales & Seaton, 1826.

United States. Cong. Senate. *Journal of the Senate of the United States of America Being the Third Session of the Twenty-Fifth Congress, Begun and Held at the City of Washington December 3, 1838.* Washington, D.C.: Blair and Rives, 1838.

CHAPTER 2

Hazel Green (KY) Herald. "Kentucky's Eloquent Young Orator." 2 Jun. 1886.

————. "State News." 11 Mar. 1885: 1.

Hillsboro (OH) News Herald. "National Dudes: Congressmen Who Are Most Careful of Their Dress." 29 Dec. 1887.

Louisville (KY) Times. "Kentucky's Silver-Tongued Taulbee Caught in Flagrante." 11 Dec. 1887.

Maysfield (KY) Daily Bulletin. "Adjacent Counties: Vanceburg, Lewis Counties." 24 Jul. 1884: 3.

Mt. Airy (KY) Sentinel Democrat. "Taulbee Shot." 7 Mar. 1890.

New York Times. "Charles E. Kincaid Is Dead." 3 Nov. 1906.

————. "Death of Mr. Taulbee." 11 Mar. 1890.

Stanford (KY) Semi-Weekly Interior Journal. "W.P. Walton." 4 Sep. 1888: 2.

Washington Critic. "Murder: Taulbee Shot." 28 Feb. 1890.

Washington Post. "Admission of Threats." 29 Mar. 1891: 6.

————. "Explained by a Skull." 26 Mar. 1891: 11.

————. "Indicted for Murder." 15 Mar. 1891: 1.

————. "Investigation the Scandal." 10 Dec. 1887: 3.

————. "Kincaid Is Not Guilty." 9 Apr. 1891: 1.

————. "Laura L. Jeffords." 27 Dec. 1959: E10.

————. "Men Who Quit Congress." 25 Feb. 1889: 6.

————. "Mr. Taulbee Is Dead." 12 Mar. 1890: 1.

————. "Nearly a Fatal Shot." 1 Mar. 1890: 4.

————. "With Masonic Honors." 14 Mar. 1890: 2.

CHAPTER 3

Bohlen, Celestine. "Bomb Blast Rips Room in Capitol." *Washington Post*, 8 Nov. 1983: A1.

Boykin, Edward. *Congress and the Civil War.* New York: McBride, 1955.

Briggs, Emily Edson. "The Dragons of the Lobby." *The Olivia Letters.* Washington, D.C.: Neale, 1906.

Britton, Nan. *The President's Daughter.* New York: The Elizabeth Ann Guild, 1927.

Buel, James William. *Mysteries and Miseries of America's Great Cities.* St. Louis, MO: Historical Publishing, 1883.

Dionne, E.J., Jr. "The Elusive Front-Runner: Gary Hart." *New York Times Magazine*, 3 May 1987: SM28.

Harsha, David Addison. *The Life of Charles Sumner.* New York: Dayton and Burdick, 1856.

Laurens (SC) Advertiser. "Tillman and M'Laurin." 26 Feb. 1902: 1.

Mencken, Henry Louis, and Peter W. Dowell, ed. *"Ich Kuss die Hand": The Letters of H.L. Mencken to Gretchen Hood.* Tuscaloosa: University of Alabama Press, 1986.

McGee, Jim, and Tom Fiedler. "Miami Woman Is Linked to Hart Candidate Denies Any Impropriety." *Miami Herald*, 3 May 1987: 1A.

McGee, Jim, Tom Fiedler, James Savage "The Gary Hart Story: How It Happened." *Miami Herald*, 10 May 1987.

National Republican (Washington, D.C.). "Frightful Explosion at the Capitol." 20 May 1876.

New Lisbon (OH) Anti-Slavery Bugle. "News of the Week." 19 Jul. 1856: 3.

New York Daily Tribune. "Assault on Senator Sumner." 23 May 1856: 5.

————. "Doings in Congress." 29 May 1856: 4.

New York Times. "Bomb Exploded in the Capitol." 3 Jul. 1915.

————. "Gas Explosion in the Capitol." 20 May 1876.

————. "His Letters Expose Holt." 4 Jul. 1915:1

————. "Set an Infernal Machine." 4 Jul. 1915:1

Parker, Dorothy. "An American Du Barry." *The Portable Dorothy Parker.* New York: Penguin Books, 1976. Originally published in the *New Yorker*, October 15, 1927.

Poore, Benjamin Perley. *Reminiscences of Sixty Years in the National Metropolis.* Philadelphia: Hubbard Brothers, 1886.

Robenalt, James. *The Harding Affair: Love and Espionage During the Great War.* New York: Palgrave Macmillan, 2009.

Sumner, Charles. *Defense of Massachusetts.* Washington, D.C.: Buell & Blanchard, 1854.

———. *The Kansas Question: Senator Sumner's Speech.* Cincinnati, OH: Blanchard, 1856.

United States. Cong. Senate. "Bomb Explodes in Capitol." http://www.senate.gov.

———. *Senate Manual.* Washington, D.C.: GPO, 1903

Washington Herald. "Lindbergh Wants Senate Abolished." 23 Mar. 1912: 6.

Washington Times. "Capitol Not Fire-Proof." 8 Nov. 1898: 7.

———. "Capitol Was in Danger." 7 Nov. 1898.

Chapter 4

Bates, David Homer. *Lincoln in the Telegraph Office.* New York: The Century Co., 1907.

Bradlee, Ben. "Even Addresses Are Wrong: Capital the Victim of Sloppy Reporting." *Washington Post*, 4 Mar. 1951: B7.

Evening Critic (Washington, D.C.). "The Remains of Sergeant Cross: His Family Opposed to Disturbing Them." 15 Aug. 1884: 1.

Greely, Adolphus W. *Three Years of Arctic Service: An Account of the Lady Franklin Bay Expedition of 1881–84 and the Attainment of the Farthest North.* New York: Scribner's, 1894.

Hendrickson, Robert. *The Facts On File Dictionary of American Regionalisms.* New York: Facts On File, 2000.

Lait, Jack, and Lee Mortimer. *Washington Confidential.* New York: Crown, 1951.

Moffat, R. Burnham. *The Barclays of New York: Who They Are and Who They Are Not,—and Some Other Barclays.* New York: Robert Grier Cooke, 1904.

Morrissey, USMC Major (Ret.) Robert B. "My Memories of Marine Sergeant George C. Scott." 24 Sep. 1999. http://www.angelfire.com/ca4/gunnyg/gcscott.html.

National Republican (Washington, D.C.). "Not Cannibals: The Horrible Story About the Greely Party Denied." 13 Aug. 1884: 1.

———. "Toward the North Pole: A Washington Boy's Experience in the Arctic Regions." 29 Oct. 1881.

National Tribune (Washington, D.C.). "Miscellaneous." 16 Jul. 1885.

New York Times. "Horrors of Camp Sabine: Terrible Story of Greely's Dreary Camp." 12 Aug. 1884.

Price, Major H. Brooks, and William M. Rittenhouse. "Maple Square: 630 South Carolina Avenue, S.E." *Historic American Buildings Survey.* Washington, D.C., 1983.

Vermont Phoenix. "Deplorable Suicide." 25 Sep. 1845.

Washington Post. "An Arctic Hero Rests: Five Thousand People Gather at the Grave of Sergeant Cross." 11 Aug. 1884: 1.

———. "Drink-Food Ratio Is Key to ABC Case." 26 Jul. 1949: B1.

———. "Fanciulli a Prisoner: Bandmaster and Lieutenant Clash Over Authority." 1 Jun. 1897: 1.

———. "Ordeal for Fanciulli: Summary Court of Inquiry to Convene Today." 11 Jun. 1897:1.

———. "Sentence Too Severe: Court-martial Verdict of Dismissal Set Aside." 23 Jun. 1897:2.

———. "Will It Be a Reprimand?" 15 Jun. 1897:12.

CHAPTER 5

Anderson, Jack. "J. Edgar Hoover—An Assessment." *Washington Post,* 3 May 1972: B15.

Baker, Jean H. *The Stevensons: A Biography of an American Family.* New York: W.W. Norton, 1996.

Baltimore Sun. "CCC Worker Killed, Two Others Wounded in Battle at Tavern." 23 Apr. 1934: 1.

———. "15 U.S. Agents Kill Dillinger." 23 Jul. 1934: 1.

———. "Only 30, Succeeds Burns in Government Bureau." 26 Dec. 1924: 1.

Briggs, Ellis. *Proud Servant: The Memoirs of a Career Ambassador.* Kent, OH: Kent State University Press, 1998.

Church, Frank. *Supplementary Detailed Staff Reports on Intelligence Activities and the Rights of Americans, Book III: Final Report of the Select Committee to Study Governmental Operations with Respect to Intelligence Activities.* Washington, D.C.: USGPO, 1976.

Coben, Stanley. *A. Mitchell Palmer: Politician.* New York: Da Capo, 1972.

Evening Public Ledger (Philadelphia). "Wilson Moves Against Espionage Activities." 19 Nov. 1917.

Gentry, Curt. *J. Edgar Hoover: The Man and the Secrets*. New York: W.W. Norton, 1991.

Greider, William. "Analysis of Stolen FBI Documents Provides Glimpse of Bureau at Work: Analysis of Stolen Records Gives Glimpse of FBI at Work." *Washington Post*, 4 Jul. 1971: A1.

———. "J. Edgar Hoover Dies Quietly at Home." *Washington Post*, 3 May 1972: A1.

Johnson, David Alan. *Betrayal: The True Story of J. Edgar Hoover and the Nazi Saboteurs Captured During WWII*. New York: Hippocrene, 2007.

Marder, Murrey. "Senator Is Flayed for Seeking to Link Law Firm Aide with Communists." *Washington Post*, 10 Jun. 1954: 1.

McCarthy, Joe. *McCarthyism: The Fight for America*. New York: Devin-Adair, 1952.

Morello, Carol. "FBI Agents Upset over Movie Alleging J. Edgar Hoover Was Gay." *Washington Post*, 29 Nov. 2011.

Nash, Jay Robert. *Citizen Hoover: A Critical Study of the Life and Times of J. Edgar Hoover*. Lanham, MD: Rowman & Littlefield, 1972.

New York Times. "Mrs. Roosevelt Says M'Carthy Is Menace." 21 Sep. 1951.

———. "Will Reorganize Department." 1 Mar. 1933.

New York Tribune. "Anarchist Leaders Fought to Last Legal Ditch to Escape Deportation." 22 Dec. 1919.

Schrecker, Ellen. *Many Are the Crimes*. Princeton, NJ: Princeton University Press, 1998.

Summers, Anthony. *Official and Confidential: The Secret Life of J. Edgar Hoover*. New York: Putnam, 1993.

Theoharis, Athan G., and John Stuart Cox. *The Boss: J. Edgar Hoover and the Great American Inquisition*. N.p., n.d.

United States. Federal Bureau of Investigation. "Eleanor Roosevelt" vault. fbi.gov/Eleanor Roosevelt.

———. "Subject: James Francis Cagney." vault.fbi.gov/James Cagney/.

Washington Post. "Trap Fails as Dillinger Shoots Way to Freedom" 1 Apr. 1934: 1.

Washington Times. "Blast at Palmer Home Second in Capital Since Beginning of World War." 3 Jun. 1919: 3.

———. "Official List of Washington Men Registered for War Service June 5th at Precincts 4-C and 5-A" 26 Jun. 1917: 8.

———. "School Year Ends This Afternoon." 18 Jun. 1913: 16.

CHAPTER 6

Carlson, Peter. "Tale from the Crypt." *Washington Post*, 20 Oct. 2005.

Evening Critic (Washington, D.C.). "Suicide by Laudanum." 14 Nov. 1881.

Evening Star (Washington, D.C.). "Dead Bodies in a Buggy: Resurrectionists Surprised by a Policeman Last Night." 21 Dec. 1889.

———. "The Last of Beau Hickman: An Original Character Gone." 1 Sep. 1873.

———. "Mary Ann Hall." 31 Jan. 1886.

———. "Who Are the Grave Robbers?" 24 Dec. 1889.

L'Enfant, Peter. *Plan of the City Intended for the Permanent Seat of the Government of t[he] United States. Computer-assisted reproduction of Pierre Charles L'Enfant's 1791 manuscript plan for the city of Washington, produced by the U.S. Geological Survey for the Library of Congress.* Washington, D.C.: Library of Congress, 1991.

National Republican (Washington, D.C.). "Beau Hickman Dying: Sketch of an Eventful Career." 2 Sep. 1873.

———. "District Supreme Court—Criminal Term: Judge Olin." 20 Feb. 1864.

———. "Outraging the Dead: Beau Hickman Resurrected." 4 Sep. 1873.

———. "Resurrectionists: Two Dead Bodies Found in a Box." 11 Nov. 1874.

New York Times. "Grave-Robber Christian." 21 Nov. 1878.

———. "Robert L. Hickman: 'Beau' Hickman." 3 Sep. 1873.

Repertory & General Advertiser (Boston, MA). "The Gerry-mander: A New Species of Monster, Which Appeared in Essex South District in January Last." 27 Mar. 1812.

Shultz, Suzanne M. *Body Snatching: The Robbing of Graves for the Education of Physicians in Early Nineteenth Century America.* Jefferson, NC: McFarland and Co., 2005.

Smithsonian Institution. *Archeological Investigations: National Museum of the American Indian Site Washington, D.C.* Washington, D.C.: Smithsonian Institution, 1997.

Trollope, Frances. *Domestic Manners of the Americans.* London: Whittaker, Treacher and Co., 1832.

United States. Cong. Senate. "History of the Congressional Cemetery." *Senate Documents: 59th Congress, 2nd Session, Vol. 2.* Washington, D.C.: GPO, 1907.

United States. Cong. *Supplement to the Revised Statutes of the United States Vol. 2 No. 6 1895–1896.* Washington, D.C.: GPO, 1896.

Valentine, Paul W., and Avis Thomas-Lester. "Cult Ties Suspected in Church, Grave Thefts." *Washington Post*, 16 Jun. 1991: C16.

Washington Post. "A Grave Robber's Exploits: Some of the Stories Which Are Told of Jensen, the Resurrectionist." 4 Dec. 1880.

————. "Grave Robber's Trial." 7 Jun. 1890: 8.

————. "Her Second Funeral: A Sad Procession Follows Mrs. Cheek's Body to the Despoiled Grave." 23 Dec. 1889.

————. "'The Resurrectionist King': A Ridiculous Attempt to Popularize Body-Snatching." 19 May 1884: 4.

Washington Times. "Hymns Mingle with Orgies." 17 Feb. 1895.

Watterston, George. *A Picture of Washington*. Washington, D.C.: William M. Morrison, 1840.

CHAPTER 7

Beymer, William Gilmore. *On Hazardous Service: Scouts and Spies of the North and South*. New York: Harper and Brothers, 1912.

Claiborne, William. "ACLU Study Disputed by Jail Officials." *Washington Post*, 18 Mar. 1972: D1.

Cross, Carolyn. "Almshouse Inmates Move to Blue Plains." *Washington Post*, 25 Sep. 1906: 9.

Dowling, Harry Filmore. *City Hospitals: The Undercare of the Underprivileged*. Cambridge, MA: Harvard University Press, 1982.

Greenhow, Rose O'Neal. *My Imprisonment and the First Year of Abolition Rule at Washington*. London: Richard Bentley, 1863.

Johnson, Haynes. "Jail Rebels Free All Hostages." *Washington Post*, 12 Oct. 1971: A1.

Moore, Irna. "City Plans to Build 2 New Jails Here." *Washington Post*, 17 Jun. 1971: D1.

Mosby, John Singleton. *The Memoirs of Colonel John S. Mosby*. Boston: Little, Brown, 1917.

National Republican (Washington, D.C.). "Blockade Runners." 20 Feb. 1864.

————. "Condition of the Work-House." 28 Nov. 1877: 1.

————. "Council Proceedings: Board of Alderman." 17 Mar. 1868: 2.

————. "Crazy to Fight." 2 Nov. 1862.

————. "Execution of Henry Wirz: The Andersonville Jailor Expiates His Crimes on the Gallows." 10 Nov. 1865 (Second Edition): 2.

————. "From the Grand Army: The Grand Review." 9 Oct. 1861.

————. "Rebel Prisoners." 6 Aug. 1862: 2.

National Tribune (Washington, D.C.). "The Assassin Hanged: Guiteau Pays the Penalty of His Crime on the Scaffold." 8 Jul. 1882: 5.

New York Times. "The Attempt to Kill Guiteau: Sergt. Mason Sorry That He Did Not Succeed in His Object." 13 Sep. 1881.

————. "Expiation: Charles Guiteau Hanged for the Murder of the President." 1 Jul. 1882: 1.

————. "Sergt. Mason's Sentence." 11 Mar. 1882.

Philadelphia Evening Telegraph. "A Convict Killed." 20 Apr. 1869.

Ramirez, Paul. "Penal System Turning Corner." *Washington Post,* 13 Sep. 1973: A41.

Robinson, Timothy S. "Gordon Liddy Freed on Bond After 21 Months in Jail." *Washington Post,* 16 Oct. 1974: A16.

Stokes, Dillard. "One Nazi Who Informed on Others Gets Life Term, Second 30 Years; Doomed Six Are Given Scant Notice." *Washington Post,* 9 Aug. 1942: 1.

United States. Cong. House. *Report of the Commissioners of the District of Columbia December 7, 1874.* Washington, D.C.: GPO, 1874.

United States. Cong. Senate. "The Report of the Commissioners Appointed to Investigate the Jail, Workhouse, etc., in the District of Columbia." Congressional Edition, Vol. 5407. Washington, D.C.: GPO, 1908.

Valentine, Paul W. "$30 Million Jail Opens in District." *Washington Post,* 30 Mar. 1976: C1.

Washington Times. "An Hour Among the Workhouse Prisoners." 29 Mar. 1903: 3.

Washington Times Magazine. "How the Workhouse in Washington Sometimes Makes Good Women Out of Bad." 23 Dec. 1906: 9.

Whiteford, Mary Noyes. "Occoquan a Paradise Compared with Refuge of Cut's Ill and Needy." *Washington Times,* 13 Mar. 1916: 1.

About the Author

R obert Pohl is a stay-at-home dad, tour guide and author. He has previously written a book on the history of his house, as well as a book looking at the emancipation of the slaves in the District of Columbia. He writes a regular column for both the *Hill Rag* and the *Hill Is Home*.

Pohl began as a computer programmer but gave that up for a more eclectic lifestyle. When not playing with his son, touring eighth graders through Washington or writing, Pohl volunteers at his local library and his son's school.

Robert Pohl lives on Capitol Hill with his wife, son and two cats.

Photo by Ian Herzog-Pohl.

Visit us at
www.historypress.net